# POWERED BY PURPOSE

## *Discover **Why** You Are*

ISBN 978-1-621660-81-1

Published by CSA Publishing,
a department of XP Ministries
PO Box 1017, Maricopa, AZ., 85139
XPpublishing.com
For Worldwide Distribution

# POWERED BY PURPOSE

*Discover **Why** You Are*

## Daniel H. Park

**Other books**

**by**

**Daniel H. Park**

*Never Burn Out*:
*Discover the Reality of Your Identity*

*Lost in Jesus*:
*30 Days of Deeper Intimacy with Jesus*

*Step into Destiny*:
*Find & Fulfill Your God-given Purpose*

## DEDICATED TO:

MY MOM, DAD, AND SISTER for always believing in my purpose and being so supportive.

EVERY MENTOR who has invested in me and helped me to find, develop, and fulfill my purpose.

DR. MYLES MUNROE, whose teachings on the Kingdom and personal purpose have transformed the way I see myself, others, life, and the world. I could not write this book apart from your mentorship.

# CONTENTS

# FOREWORD

by

**Dr. Myles Munroe**

I have come to the conclusion that the two most important questions in life are: Who am I and why am I here?

If these questions are not answered successfully, then life on planet Earth will be an experiment and an investment in disillusionment and frustration.

If you don't know who you are you are, why you exist, and what your purpose is in life, then you are destined to become an imitation of someone else. The question of personal purpose has been the objective of ancient civilizations and has produced a myriad of philosophical and religious prospects, which continue to exercise the attention of mankind today.

This erudite, eloquent, and immensely thought provoking work gets to the heart of this nagging human dilemma of discovery of personal purpose and unveils some of the deepest passions and aspirations of the human heart the search for true meaning in life.

This is an indispensable read for anyone who wants to live life above the norm and fulfill their personal purpose on earth. This is a profound authoritative work, which spans the collective wisdom of the ages and yet breaks new ground in its approach.

This exceptional work by Daniel Park is one of the most profound, practical, principle-centered approaches to the subject of self-discovery and identity I have read in a long time. The author's approach to this timely and critical issue of purpose brings a fresh breath of air that captivates the heart, engages the mind, and inspires the spirit of the reader.

The author's ability to reduce complex theories to simple and practical self-discovery principles that the least among us can understand is amazing. This work simplifies the soul searching process and delivers profound truths with exceptional clarity.

Daniel's approach awakens the untapped inhibiters that retard the power of our personal purpose, and his antidotes empower us to rise above these self-defeating, self-limiting factors to a life of exploits in spiritual and mental advancement!

Daniel also integrates time-tested precepts into each chapter, giving each principle a practical application, which makes the entire process people friendly.

I enjoyed the mind expanding experience of reading this exciting book. I admonish you to plunge into this ocean of knowledge, and watch your life change for the better as you experience the power of discovering your purpose and reason in life!

DR. MYLES MUNROE

International Motivational Speaker,
USA Today Best-selling Author,
Chairman, BFM International, ITWLA
Nassau, Bahamas

# 1

# Why are You?

Think about these five questions:

## 1. How are you?

You probably get this one asked daily. Some of us respond with words like good, fine, I'm all right, or can't complain without even thinking about it. But to really answer this question, you would need to explain how you are doing circumstantially, physically, relationally, emotionally, and spiritually. It's not the hardest question to answer because we have our opinions about how we are faring in these categories.

## 2. Where are you?

You may be reading this book in Asia, South America, or Africa. Perhaps your on an airplane, in your room, at the park, or even on the beach. I think you know where you are so this question usually doesn't take much research or introspection to answer. Thanks to technology, if you wanted to get really specific, you could just touch some buttons on your Smartphone or GPS system and find out the exact latitude and longitude of your current location.

## 3. What are you?

Talk about an open-ended question! How would you answer? We often define ourselves with one of these ten characteristics:

- Name
- Age
- Gender
- Occupation

- Race
- Social class
- Assets
- Martial status
- Education
- Physicality

All three of the previous questions are much easier to answer than our next question:

### 4. Why are you?

I believe that this is the most important question you can answer about yourself, but it also seems to be the most confusing to people. The answer to this very personal question cannot be easily retrieved from a Google search. Your Smartphone is not smart enough to answer this question. Even the best of academia cannot impart this information.

This question delves much deeper than our first three considerations. For although biology can teach you *what* you are made of, it cannot explain *why* you were made. It's not difficult to identify your *race*, but have you identified your *reason*? You probably know the *day* you were born, but do you know *why* you were born? You

17

might be able to write down your *occupation*, but can you write down the original purpose for your existence? It's not hard to describe your *physicality*, but can you describe your *purpose*?

Only when you can answer, "Why are you?" will you be able to answer this next question:

## 5. Who are you?

*What* you are doesn't determine your identity, because your "who" is determined by *why* you are. The next few chapters will seek to support that bold statement, but let me close this chapter by asking:

Would you agree that your *eternal significance* is not found in the temporary "stuff" that you have accumulated?

Would you agree that *deep meaning* in your life can't be found in the surface level of your appearance?

Would you agree that the *immeasurable value* of your soul does not come from the measurable assets you have under your name?

Would you agree that *your importance* is not wrapped up in your age, occupation, or skin color, but in the essence of who you are?

Your *worth* comes from the fact that your Creator made you one of a kind with special purpose. Therefore, your identity cannot be found in *what* you are, but *why* you are.

I may not know *how* you are doing, *where* you are reading this, or *what* your age, gender, or occupation is, but I am fully convinced that your *why* exists in the heart of the Creator. I pray this book will lead you into the Creator's heart, where you will find your original purpose... and your identity: *why* you are and *who* you are.

 **MEDITATION**

Why is your identity so much deeper than how you are presently doing, where you currently live, and the ten characteristics of your what?

# 2

# Your WHY Preceded Your WHAT

Just as a book already existed in the mind of the author before it hit the bookstores, your *why* was already penned in the mind of the Creator before your *what* appeared on the shelf of Planet Earth.

Let me introduce you to the Creator. You are too beautiful, wonderful, intelligent, creative, and gifted to be the blind product of chance. You are the work of art of a divine being, whom we will call the Creator.

The Creator is greater than us because we came from Him; He did not come from us. When someone makes you a delicious meal, you don't thank the meal for the chef, but it's fitting to thank the chef for the meal, for the chef is the source. The Creator is your Ultimate Source and therefore He's greater than you.

In the same way, your *why* is the source of your *what*. Your *what* came from your *why* and therefore your *why* is greater than your *what*. The only reason you even exist is because you first had a *purpose*. Thus, your identity does not come from your *what*, but rather from your *why*.

Jeremiah was an acclaimed Jewish prophet who lived long ago. Under divine inspiration, he explained that his why existed before his what:

> The word of the Lord came to me, saying, "Before I formed you in the womb I knew you, before you were born I set you apart; I appointed you as a prophet to the nations."

"Ah, Sovereign Lord," I said, "I do not know how to speak; I am only a child."

But the Lord said to me, "Do not say, 'I am only a child.' You must go to everyone I send you to and say whatever I command you. Do not be afraid of them, for I am with you and will rescue you," declares the Lord.

— Jeremiah 1:4-8 NIV

Notice how the Creator predetermined Jeremiah's purpose before he even entered the womb of his mother. You might be thinking, "Well, that's probably just Jeremiah. The Creator didn't put that much thought into the rest of us."

Really? You actually believe that our Almighty Creator is that limited? The Holy Bible reveals that the Creator is no respecter of persons (see Acts 10:34). He put the same amount of thought and purpose into all of us. The tragedy is that not all of us know and believe in our purpose to the same degree!

Solomon was one of the wisest kings from the pages of history, and he wrote, "To every *thing there is* a season, and a time to every purpose under the heaven" (Ecclesiastes 3:1 KJV). According to this wise proverb, it's because the Creator has a purpose for you that He sent you into time!

The reason you entered your mother's womb at the specific time you did was because your purpose was for that very appointed time. Your purpose is too dynamic and compelling to have just remained in the heart and mind of the Creator! You needed to be given a platform – the platform of time. Earth is your timeshare.

## THE ARCHITECT OF PURPOSE

The Creator is not a sporadic artist who accidentally ends up with an abstract piece of art. He's an on-purpose architect who has all the blueprints penned before construction begins. The very construction of your genetic code is proof that your heavenly blueprints were already determined.

When you picture the architecture of a McDonald's, you probably think about a drive-thru that goes around the restaurant, a kitchen in the back, and the seating area in the front. The reason the McDonald's branch was designed that way was because its purpose was already determined. The structure of the facility was custom-made for the purpose of being a fast-food restaurant with a drive-thru. You, too, were designed specifically for a purpose; it's no coincidence that you have the natural gifts and talents that you possess. The Creator knew exactly what He was doing when He fabricated you in the womb.

The Creator has a habit of beginning with the end in mind. Isaiah, another Jewish prophet who often heard the Creator's voice, penned:

> Declaring the end from the beginning
> and from ancient times things not yet
> done, saying, "My counsel shall stand,
> and I will accomplish all my purpose."

> — Isaiah 46:10

The Creator creates something after He has already determined its destiny. Destiny precedes conception. Now matter how you were conceived you are not a mistake! Don't ever say that the Creator doesn't have a special destiny for you, because your conception proves otherwise.

## PURPOSE VS. DESTINY

What is the difference between purpose and destiny? While purpose is the **why** the Creator made you and gave you life, destiny is **where** the Creator wants to take you in life.

To successfully reach your destiny, you must know your purpose. Understanding your purpose is vital to effectively walk in your destiny. Fulfilling destiny is the result of mastering your purpose. To reject your purpose is to miss your destiny. They function as two sides to the same coin.

 **MEDITATION**

How is your conception proof that you have a purpose and a destiny?

# 3

# Your WHY
# will Overcome

He had a nasty speech impediment, a haunting criminal record, and no experience in politics or the military. Yet, he led three million Jews out of slavery. His name is Moses.

He grew up in the ghetto, and His siblings never thought He would amount to much. In those days, most carpenters' sons took over their dad's business and died a carpenter. Though He did not study under the tutelage of the top rabbi's of His day, He became the most famous rabbi this world has ever known. Billions worship this Man today. His name is Jesus of Nazareth.

Do you feel under-qualified for greatness? Believing in your purpose will cause you to break out of the prison cell of restrictions. Your eternal purpose will overpower your temporary setbacks.

You might not have the ideal list of *what* you are, but here is good news: your *why* is greater than all the present limitations of your *what* (for the reference of *what* you are, see chapter one).

## Feeling Unqualified?

After the Creator communicated His grand purposes for the young prophet (Jeremiah 1:4), Jeremiah felt unqualified because of *what* he was. Listen to his response to the Creator:

> "Ah, Sovereign Lord," I said, "I do not know how to speak; I am only a child."
>
> But the Lord said to me, "Do not say, 'I am only a child.' You must go

to everyone I send you to and say whatever I command you. Do not be afraid of them, for I am with you and will rescue you," declares the Lord.

— Jeremiah 1:5-8 NIV

We need to recognize that our feelings are often subjective and not reliable discerners of truth; therefore, I'm thankful for another Source. Do you see how the Creator wanted to make sure Jeremiah understood that his *why* was greater than the limitations of his *what*?

The Creator was communicating to Jeremiah that his *circumstances* could not stop his *purpose*. Although Jeremiah did *not* have the right *age*, the ideal *occupation*, the fancy *education*, or the seasoned and respectable *physicality*, the Creator's purpose would overpower all of these limitations. But just as Jeremiah had to believe, you, too, must believe the promise that your *why* will overpower the limitations of your *what*.

The Apostle Paul told his young protégé, Timothy, "Don't let anyone look down on you because you are young" (1 Timothy 4:12). The seasoned mentor was saying that if people try to look down on you because you don't have the right *what*, make sure that you don't let that get to you! God's purposes for your life are greater!

The New Testament Scriptures read, "There is neither Jew nor Greek, there is neither slave nor free, there is no male and female, for you are all one in Christ Jesus" (Galatians 3:28). Essentially, this verse tells you that nobody should write you off because of your race, occupation, or gender.

Just because you grew up in poverty, it doesn't mean you have to die in poverty. Gideon came from the lowest social class and was even the runt of his family. He lived a low life. The turnaround in his life happened when an angel showed up to Gideon and called him a mighty man of valor (see Judges 6:12). The angel went on to reveal his divine purpose, and Gideon became a new man.

The Creator wanted Gideon to see himself in light of his divine purpose, not his problems and limitations. By grasping hold of his *why*, Gideon went from the bottom of the social ladder to become one of the greatest leaders in Israel's history. But this could not have happened unless he saw himself in light of his purpose.

You will live a low life until you get high on your divine purpose. Your purpose is better than any drug. Once you find it, you will start having some *real* fun!

You may have been the black sheep of your family, slimed by rejection and stabbed with mistreatment by the very ones who should have loved you the most. There is still great purpose on the inside of you!

## JUST ASK KING DAVID

Some Bible scholars believe that David was born out of wedlock and that this caused his father to esteem his brothers above him since David reminded his father of failure and shame. This is further evidenced because David looked different than his brothers (see 1 Samuel 16:12), and he candidly wrote in his memoirs, "Behold, I was brought forth in iniquity, and in sin did my mother conceive me" (Psalm 51:5). Perhaps that is why David's father, Jesse, hid David when the prophet Samuel came to his house, because Samuel represented the Creator's purity.

But, nevertheless, in the midst of all this dysfunction, David still declared his eternal value by stating:

For you formed my inward parts; you knitted me together in my mother's womb. I praise you, for I am fearfully and wonderfully made. Wonderful are your works; my soul knows it very well.

— Psalm 139:13-14

David was empowered by his purpose.

## THEY MIGHT DESPISE YOU NOW

When Nathanael heard that the Jewish Messiah had come out of Nazareth, he asked the blunt question, "Can anything good come out of Nazareth?"

Philip replied, "Come and see" (John 1:46). People generally didn't link potential and greatness with such a rundown town as Nazareth. Yet, it doesn't matter what the general consensus is! The Creator's purpose overrides the general consensus.

When Nathanael saw Jesus the Rabbi manifest His purpose, his view of the Nazarene radically changed. He declared, "Rabbi, you are the Son of God; you are the King of Israel" (John 1:49).

Like Jesus, people might despise you when they learn about your *what*, but when they see you manifest your purpose, they will be blown away. They will see the dynamic leader within you!

Some people think that following Jesus Christ will restrict their lives, but the very opposite is true. He is the perfect example of an overcomer who fulfilled His divine purpose, and He turns His followers into overcomers who fulfill *their* divine purposes!

While your parents played a part in your *what*, the Creator single-handedly determined your *why*. My parents determined my name, appearance, race, social class, etc. But the Creator alone determined my purpose. Your purpose will prevail and overcome every obstacle, because it is one hundred percent divine!

 **MEDITATION**

What are some of the most challenging aspects of your life? Why should you believe that your purpose will overcome all of those challenges?

# 4

# Your WHAT is
# Your Tool

Stevie Wonder's keyboard is not greater than him: it's just his instrument. Tiger Woods' golf clubs aren't worth more than him: they are only his equipment. Kobe Bryant's basketball is worth forty dollars, while he is worth millions, the ball is merely his tool. Celine Dion's microphone can cost thousands of dollars, but she is far more valuable than her mic, because her mic is just her vehicle. Your *what* is a simply an instrument, equipment, a tool, or a vehicle for your *why*.

We should take care of our health for the purpose of fulfilling our purpose. We should dress presentably so our *what* can help our *why,* instead of hindering it. Education can assist our purpose, but your *why* is not found in your *what*! Your *what* isn't you any more than Tiger Woods' golf club is Tiger Woods.

If you equate your *why* to your *what* and try to find your significance in your stuff, your life will be in disorder. If you think your tools equal you, you will experience the following disorders.

## THE DISORDER OF OBSESSION

You will be obsessed over your body image if you think that your significance is in your weight or physique. It's sad to see people who become addicted to plastic surgery because they find their value in their appearance.

If your identity is your *what*, you will be obsessed over popularity, success, your pets, cars, etc. Some have lost purpose for living when their popularity has gone, their pets die, or the car is totaled. That's a true disorder.

Those who find their identity in *what* they have are obsessed over money, since they believe that the worth of their soul is found in the size of their bank account. The Holy Bible teaches that the love of money is the root of all evil (see 1 Timothy 6:10). In other words, obsession over money leads to many other disorders.

## THE DISORDER OF DEPRESSION

Obsession leads to depression. People get depressed because they were first obsessed over their *what*. Imagine getting happy or depressed based upon your current prestige, your most recent performance, or your latest possessions. That's an emotional roller coaster! Depression is a disorder that can happen when we think our *what* equals our *why*.

## THE DISORDER OF RACISM

Adolf Hitler believed and preached that your *what* determined your *why*. He brainwashed many to accept that some were born to rule, while others were destined for destruction. This led to the horrific tragedy of the holocaust.

If you think that your significance is found in your skin color, you will be filled with pride or shame because of your race. Your *race* is for your *reason*, but your *reason* is not found in your *race*. Your *race* serves your *reason*; it doesn't own it.

Now for most of my readers, this is common sense. But why? It's because we innately know that our *why* is not found in our *what*. This is a timeless principle. Let's stay faithful to it.

Disorders such as strange obsessions, depression, and racism will always plague the life that elevates *what* above *why*. This is because it's in contradiction to the Creator's order. He already placed your *why* far above your *what*.

 **MEDITATION**

What are some tools that the Creator has given to you for the sake of fulfilling your purpose? Have you confused your tools with your identity?

# 5

# Deep Fulfillment

A person can have a PhD in human anatomy but still feel empty inside. Someone can have a famous name and stand on top of the social ladder but still feel like life is meaningless. A person can have the most coveted physique but feel empty inside because they don't know their *purpose*. It's not knowing *what* you are that will fulfill you.

King Solomon had it all when it came to stuff and status. He overdosed on more physical pleasure than anyone. He had more toys than Donald Trump, more women than Hugh Hefner, and more money than Bill Gates. His wisdom and accomplishments were matchless. Even with all of this, his commentary on life was:

> "Meaningless! Meaningless!" says the Teacher. "Everything is meaningless!"
>
> — Ecclesiastes 12:8 NIV

Solomon concluded that the only solution for the problem of emptiness was to connect with the Source of our purpose and live according to His blueprints for our lives. He concludes his book, which is titled *Ecclesiastes,* by writing:

> Now all has been heard; here is the conclusion of the matter: Fear God [Get to intimately know the Author of your purpose] and keep his commandments [or purposes], for this is the whole duty of man.
>
> — Ecclesiastes 12:13 NIV

Like Solomon, you can have all the stuff and status that this world has to offer and still have no sense of significance. You can further excel in your performances, store up your possessions, and soar into higher prestige, but without a sense of purpose, life remains meaningless. For your true significance doesn't come from simply improving your *what*, but from intimately knowing your *why* and then living it!

When a person has truly connected with their purpose by being connected to their Ultimate Source, they find deep fulfillment. Passion fills their heart, excitement sparkles from their eyes, and everyday is seen as a special opportunity. They fully enjoy the divine gift of life! I don't share this as a theory – it is my testimony.

## How to be Sorrowful

Jesus of Nazareth told a rich, young ruler to sell all of his possessions and follow Him. Now this man had the most coveted *what* of his day. He was a rich, young male with a fantastic job and a nice reputation. But this man was not willing to give up his *what* to follow Jesus. Moreover, we read:

> And when he [the rich, young ruler]
> heard this, he was very sorrowful: for
> he was very rich.
>
> — Luke 18:23

This man was so obsessed with his *what* that he ended up rejecting his *why*. If he chose to follow the Rabbi Jesus, he would have found his divine purpose — his *why* — because Jesus is the expert at leading lost people into divine purpose!

Learn from the rich, young ruler; don't be like him and reject what is most important! Whenever you exalt your *what* above your *why*, you will be very sorrowful because you have placed value on what is meaningless at the expense of what is priceless.

 **MEDITATION**

Can you think of someone who had many things but still lacked inner-fulfillment? Can you think of someone who might not have that much but still lives an exciting, fulfilled life?

# 6

# **Made of Purpose**

We desire to be loved because we were made for love. We desire to be influential and successful because we were made for influence and success. We desire a life that's full of purpose because we were made for purpose.

Our bodies crave water because it's made up of water. Our spirits crave purpose because we are made of purpose. Your spirit is the real you; your body is merely your shell. Your spirit is the part of you that has come directly from the Creator, the Father of spirits (Hebrews 12:9). The person who ignores his or her desire for water will become dehydrated, get sick, and eventually die. The person who ignores his or her desire for purpose and a meaningful existence will live a sick, shriveled up life until they, too, eventually die.

Many people live sick lives full of addictions, depression, and misery because their thirst for purpose is neglected. Many have even resorted to taking their own lives because they could not quench their ravenous thirst for purpose. Suicide is the result of purposelessness.

What is the opposite of suicide? Loving life! Through understanding their purpose, people will enjoy a full life! Jesus came to bring life and life more than abundant (see John 10:10). He came to impart purpose!

## THERE'S MORE TO YOUR LIFE

Do you hear your spirit crying out that there's got to be more to life than this? Pay attention to that voice – it's telling you the truth. There is a whole lot more to our design than we have realized.

Sadly, too many people will keep themselves preoccupied with having fun, trying to live comfortably, and scratching their egos. They will ignore the voice of their purpose, which is desperately calling out to them, "There is more to your life than what you are living!"

After spending fifty years having some fun, making some money, and having some of their ego scratched, they hit a "mid-life crisis." They realize that they don't have much time left and wonder why they are so empty inside. Some will think that the answer to the hole in their soul is to get a new spouse, car, and hobby. They think they have to change or upgrade *what* they have and instead, they really need to start fulfilling *why* they are!

The bird was purposed to fly so the Designer equipped the bird with the unique capability of flight. One ignorant bird never spread his wings to fly and became very depressed without knowing why. He thought, "I feel so empty and I don't know why; maybe I just need to eat more." That obese bird died of high blood pressure.

This is a picture of how some humans live their lives. They don't ever exercise their God-given purpose but keep thinking that what they really need is to devour more money, eat more entertainment, digest more thrills, etc. But just because you feed your fleshly appetites to new extremes doesn't mean the emptiness in your heart will dissipate. You need to spread the wings of your purpose and fly into your God-given destiny!

## PROVISION FOR THE PANT

There is provision for all of our natural desires.

We pant for food and water, and the Life Giver has supplied provision for that need. There is more than enough food and clean water in the world if we just learn to share.

We pant for sleep, and there is a satisfying solution for this craving; many people spend eight hours a day indulging in this satisfaction.

We pant for relationships, and relationships are readily available. You can be a spouse, a parent, and a friend.

We pant for beauty, and undoubtedly there is beauty to be discovered, developed, consumed, and created. As you travel, you will discover beauty. You can make art and create beauty.

For thousands of years, the sensitive soul has panted for meaning and purpose. Surely, the Creator has provided a way for us to find and fulfill that purpose.

 **MEDITATION**

Why do people pant for meaning and purpose?

# 7

# How to Abuse
# Your Life

Many people die each day from automobile accidents. This was never the intent of Henry Ford when he invented the automobile. He purposed the car to be used for transportation, not as a lethal weapon. But whenever somebody fails to honor original intent, tragedy happens.

However, the tragedies cannot erase the true purpose that was in the heart of the creator!

Car accidents are the consequence of abusing a wonderful idea. You are the Creator's wonderful idea! If our lives end in destruction, it was not the Designer's fault – it's because we abused our purpose.

The world is in the sad state it is in because we have drifted from the original purpose of the Creator. Sin literally means *to miss the mark* or, in other words: *to miss the purpose.* Humanity has turned what the Life Giver intended for blessing into a curse. Sex is intended as a blessing but some have used it to curse their own lives.

If you abuse your laptop and use it as a frying pan, it will destroy the laptop. Don't let sin destroy your life. Living in sin is like living in a trash can – nothing in the trash can fulfills its original purpose (except the trash bag). You are not a trash bag so get out of the trash can.

When Lucifer rejected his God-given purpose as an archangel, he became Satan. The angels rejected their God-given purpose and became demons. What will happen if we reject our God-given purpose?

47

## SELF-DISCOVERY WITH THE CREATOR

To refuse to believe in the Life Giver is to reject your purpose. Apart from an intelligent and loving Creator, you are the blind product of chance, and your life is a purposeless accident. You carry no reason. You are the mere consequence of a mindless, cosmic explosion. Your human soul is not any more valuable than the cockroach, since you are just a further along accident. If you don't have a Creator, you do not have a *why*; purpose and meaning are just illusions, and emptiness is reality.

This is why Solomon wrote that the only way to have meaning in your life is to "Fear God and keep his commandments [or purposes], for this is the whole duty of man" (Ecclesiastes 12:13).

What does it mean to *fear* the Creator? Does it mean to be afraid of Him and avoid Him? No. It means to honor Him and to seek Him.

A foremost, elementary way that you honor Him is to believe in Him. We must then seek Him with out hearts. Fearing God means seeking God. The Hebrew Scriptures make this clear connection.

> He set himself to **seek God** in the days of Zechariah, who instructed

him in the **fear of God**, and as long as he **sought** the LORD, God made him prosper.

— 2 Chronicles 26: 5

Afterward the children of Israel shall return and **seek the LORD their God**, and David their king, and they shall come **in fear to the LORD** and to his goodness in the latter days.

— Hosea 3:5

Did not Hezekiah **fear the LORD and seek his favor**?

— Jeremiah 26:19 NIV

As you honor the Life Giver by believing in Him, drawing nearer to Him, and inquiring of Him, He will reveal Himself to you in a more personal way (see Psalm 25:14). To be intimate with your Designer is to be intimate with your purpose, for your purpose is found in His heart – for it was founded there. Therefore, self-discovery cannot be done apart from the Creator.

In the Garden of Eden, Satan tempted Adam and Eve to eat of the tree of the knowledge of good and evil because Satan wanted them to pursue wisdom apart from the Ultimate Source of wisdom. Self-discovery apart from the Creator is often false and limited. But with the Creator, self-discovery is true and unlimited! The psalmist wrote:

> The fear of the LORD is the beginning of wisdom; all those who practice it have a good understanding.
>
> — Psalm 111:10 ESV

How are you going to operate a car to its fullest potential if you are ignorant of its capabilities and purposes? Recently, my brother-in-law let us take out his brand new, high-tech, luxury car. I was amazed at the potential of this car but, because of my lack of understanding, I did not know how to maximize the car's potential. The car ended up frustrating me more than fascinating me. Some people are more frustrated with their life than fascinated with it, because they lack self-discovery.

 **MEDITATION**

Why is self-discovery so important?

# 8

# **Purpose Maximizes Potential**

If you want to maximize the potential of your laptop computer so that it can manifest its full glory, you need to know its purpose. If you think the laptop is a doormat, you will end up destroying it. The laptop will accomplish *something*, but not the original and fullest intent of its Designer.

Studying the laptop's instruction manual will educate you about the purpose of the product. Your education will help you to maximize its capabilities. But if you violate the manual's instructions, you will destroy the product.

I believe that the Manufacturer's manual on life is the Holy Bible. This is precisely why I've made it my life's passion to study and teach this special book, because ignorance of this manual is extremely costly. The Life Giver warns, "My people are destroyed for lack of knowledge" (Hosea 4:6).

## THE KEY TO SUCCESS

Based on your purpose, there are certain things in which you cannot succeed, and there are other things in which you can easily succeed. Hard work, integrity, and a spirit of excellence are all important components to success but so is purpose.

I can work hard and pursue a basketball career, but I will not be successful. Nobody will pay me to play basketball. In fact, I have to pay the gym so I can play a game.

However, as I've been faithful to my purpose, people have offered me salaries and given me generous, personal checks. Finances do not measure success, but when we are maximizing our potential in life, we can attract provision for our needs.

We must understand our unique shape. The Creator is the potter and you are the clay (see Romans 9:21). You've been formed to serve a specific purpose, which the potter has already determined. For example, one piece of clay might be formed into a pitcher of water, while another is formed into a cooking pot. Each item can only max out their potential when they understand their potter's purpose behind their existence! If the pitcher is trying to be the pot, it will be inefficient, and there will be no demand for it.

You must operate at your highest potential! When we operate at our highest potential, the world is drawn to us. Queen Sheba traveled to Israel from Ethiopia to inquire of King Solomon, because he was operating in his purpose and potential. If Solomon had tried to make it as an Olympian or a comedian instead of perfecting his gifts of teaching, writing, and counseling, Queen Sheba would not have known that Solomon even existed.

Is there something you are working hard to develop that is just not your forte? Beware! You might end up a very poor and un-influential person. Solomon wrote, "Whoever works his land will have plenty of bread, but he who follows worthless pursuits lacks sense" (Proverbs 12:11).

You need to work your land — your purpose — and then you will have plenty. Stop trying to be something and someone you are not designed to be.

As Joseph worked his purpose by sharing his administrative and prophetic gifts, the Pharaoh came looking for him.

As Paul worked his purpose and released His full potential as a missionary, he had the audience of Caesar and other very influential people.

As Jesus Christ worked His purpose, He easily drew crowds.

Your impact will only be as great as your alignment to your purpose. You are the prodigy of *your* purpose, but the cheap imitation of anybody else's. Prodigies have simply connected with their purpose. Imitations are always much cheaper than originals. You *are* an original, so be who you *are*.

## WHO GETS THE GLORY?

When people are drawn to you, direct them to the Ultimate Source. Don't take all the glory for you. Kobe Bryant's best basketball game brings glory to him. Tiger Woods' best golf game brings glory to him. You are the Creator's best work; you are the apex of His creation so isn't it most fitting that you bring glory to Him? So, as people are amazed by you, lead them to the Life Giver so they, too, can find and fulfill their purpose and be amazing.

 **MEDITATION**

Why do you need to understand your purpose if you want to live in your full potential?

# 9

# Purpose Maximizes Fulfillment

A few years ago for my birthday, our friend Jeannie gave us a fat, orange cat named Foo – an interesting birthday present indeed! Jeannie never let Foo out of the house; he was raised indoors all seven years of his life. When Foo came to our house, he was afraid to go outside because it was so foreign to him. Yet, we encouraged him to explore the backyard.

Although he was very apprehensive at first, soon he was addicted to the great outdoors. Now, everyday he literally begs us to let him go outside so he can hunt for lizards and mice. When we try to bring him in, he rolls on his back to make it harder for us to pick him up, demanding an extra five minutes.

Though cats are divinely designed to live outdoors, Foo had been restricted. But as he got over his fears, he experienced the fulfillment of being in his element!

Like Foo, maybe your small thinking has restricted you; perhaps the negative words and treatment of others has kept you from exploring your purpose and getting into your element. I encourage you to cast off those fears, and get into your divine design! As you release your fears and receive your purpose, you will come alive. You will be addicted to being in your element.

Making a lot of money and being famous is not the guarantee of inner fulfillment; just ask the millionaire who took his own life or the celebrity who is in drug rehab. Walking in your purpose will always lead to more fulfillment than the increase of possessions or prestige.

## A WARNING

If you try to please everybody, you will never become a "somebody." If you are afraid to stand out, you will become invisible. The Creator wants to show you off, He doesn't want you to be wasted.

You can try to win everyone's approval and lose your own purpose. You can successfully become *what* your loved ones thought you should be, while failing to become who you should've been. You can try to make everyone happy but be miserable yourself.

A guitar is most fulfilled when it's making music, not when it's used as a bat. But what if everyone around you demands that the guitar be a bat, because they are obsessed with baseball? It sounds ridiculous, but it happens. For example, some parents might demand their children to become a dentist when they are actually designed to be a college professor.

The most miserable people are those who have been molded by everybody else's expectations of them so they've never grown into their preordained purpose. I'm not discounting the wisdom that our loved ones can give to us, but eat the meat and spit out the bones. Stay true to your purpose. If you are a guitar, let the world hear your music; don't smash baseballs.

 **MEDITATION**

Is somebody trying to get you to become somebody that the Creator didn't purpose you to be? Why must you stay true to your purpose?

# 10

# Purpose Maximizes Passion

There is no such thing as lazy people,
only unmotivated ones.

— John C. Maxwell

The reason why people are bored and lazy
is that they have not connected with their

purpose. When find your purpose, you will be possessed with zeal. We look up to passionate, zealous people because they are the minority; they should really be the norm.

Your passion is hidden in the package of your purpose. Unwrap your the reason for your creation, and you will discover passion – there is no greater motivator! The secret to Jesus' passion was not His personality type, but His purpose. Passionate people burn on the coals of their personal purpose.

## No Greater Joy

Purpose will bring your greatest joy. The Apostle John was one of the closest disciples of Jesus, and he confessed, "I have no greater joy than to hear that my children are walking in the truth" (3 John 1:4).

When John heard that his purpose was actualized in his sphere of influence, it gave him the greatest jolt of energy! There is no greater way to reenergize someone than to let them know that they are successfully fulfilling their God-given purpose.

I challenge you to encourage someone today who is passionately pursuing their purpose.

Share with them how their purpose has impacted your life. You have no idea how much that will bless them.

Teaching truth was so important to the Apostle John that he would have given everything he had to pursue his passion. What is that important to you? What would you be doing if you didn't have to worry about money? The answer to that question will begin to point the way to your purpose.

I understand that we need to make money, but making money should not be our number one pursuit. Those who only focus on money often miss their purpose. Don't make money your goal. Money will follow you as you pursue the Creator's design for your life. Don't put the cart before the horse – your purpose is priority.

## Passion Preserves Memories

Inside of each of us is the desire to leave a legacy. No one wants to be forgotten, nor were we designed for insignificance. We were made to so impact our world that our legacy will continue to reverberate in future generations. But who leaves that kind of legacy? One possessed with passion.

Passionless people cannot leave a legacy. They do not carry enough weight to leave a footprint – nothing remains – only a tombstone will remember their existence. This is tragic.

One passionate woman poured costly perfume at the feet of Jesus the Nazarene. In response to her radical sacrifice, Jesus prophesied, "Truly, I say to you, wherever this gospel is proclaimed in the whole world, what she has done will also be told in memory of her" (Matthew 26:13 NIV).

What ignited such ferocious passion in this woman? She was consumed with passion when she found Jesus Christ. He is "Mr. Purpose," the One who reveals purpose like no other. If you don't yet personally know Jesus, I encourage you to reach out and get to know Him. He's only a prayer away. Scripture says that *everyone* who calls on the name of the Lord will be saved (Romans 10:13).

From this woman, we learn that true passion will cause you to be remembered. Mediocre lives are not recorded in the pages of history. Only stories of relentless passion, radical living, and fearless adventures of faith are recorded in the hearts of people.

I don't remember all the twenty-dollar donations that I've given to different organizations,
because I do that on a weekly basis. But I will not
forget the two thousand-dollar donations that
my wife and I have given, because that amount
really stretched us at the time.

Passion is remembered while mediocrity is
forgotten. Some people won't even remember
their own lives because they never stepped into
the truth of their purpose. Live passionately,
stretch yourself, and make unforgettable mem-
ories!

 **MEDITATION**

Presently, what stirs the most passion in
you?

# 11

# Purpose Maximizes Time

The Creator did not purpose me to be a musician, so to spend hours a day in music lessons is a waste of time. Now, for someone else, it would be a waste of time if they did *not* take music lessons and perfect their gift!

When you waste your time, you waste your purpose. Maximize your purpose by maximizing your time – manage your time according to your purpose. When discover your purpose, you will know how to prioritize your time. My schedule will look different from yours because my purpose is different from yours.

> Many plans are in a man's mind, but it is the Lord's purpose for him that will stand.
> — Proverbs 19:21 AMP

According to this proverb, our Creator's purposes are weightier than our plans. The Life Giver blesses *His* purposes for your life. The plans you come up with for your own life are not necessarily blessed. Therefore, it's wise to plan according to the Creator's intent. This is the key to living a blessed life.

## INVEST SPARE TIME

How do you spend your spare time? When you connect with your purpose, you will invest your spare time, instead of wasting it. Our overall success is determined by what we do with our spare time.

The character and career of a young person depends on how he or she spends spare time ... The way we employ the surplus hours after provision has been made for work, meals, an sleep will determine if we develop into mediocre or powerful people.[1]

— Oswald Sanders

Don't waste your time – you were born for such a time as this (see Esther 4:14)!

 **MEDITATION**

Do you need to make changes in your time schedule to more efficiently fulfill your purpose?

---

[1] J. Oswald Sanders, *Spiritual Leadership* (Moody publishers, 1994) p. 92.

# 12

# General Purpose

We've covered the importance of purpose, but now let's define *your* purpose and look at what comprises it.

There are two kinds of purpose: **general purpose** is comprised of the Creator's original intent for all of humanity, and **specific purpose** is the Creator's unique intentions just for *you*. This chapter will deal with your general purpose.

To really understand purpose, we need to go back to the Garden of Eden, before sin distorted the Creator's original intent. Let's travel back in time to the book of Genesis – the book of beginnings – and discover the Creator's general, *fivefold* purpose for humanity.

## 1. We are created as God's children & we reflect His divine nature.

Listen into the conversation that the Creator had with Himself as He designed humanity.

> Then God said, "Let us make man in our image, after our likeness. And let them have dominion over the fish of the sea and over the birds of the heavens and over the livestock and over all the earth and over every creeping thing that creeps on the earth."
>
> — Genesis 1:26

Adam was more than the creation of the Creator; he was the son of the Creator. He had the very DNA of the Life Giver – perfect love – which He was to display (see Luke 3:38; 1 John 1:8).

One reason that superhero movies are so popular today is because they stir in us something connected to our original design. Humans with special powers fascinate us because it echoes our Creator's intent – that's us! We are children of divinity and the superheroes of Planet Earth.

## 2. We are created as powerful, dynamic leaders on this earth.

Cheetahs were fashioned to run. Eagles were made to soar. Parrots were designed to talk. Rabbits were formed to hop. Humans were made for dominion. This is why every healthy human being desires to be successful. When we are taking dominion in this world, we experience the special fulfillment of tapping into our original purpose.

The first thing God commanded Adam and Eve was to, "Be fruitful and increase in number; fill the earth and subdue it. Rule over the fish of the sea and the birds of the air and over every living creature that moves on the ground" (Genesis 1:28).

This speaks of dominion, which implies success and influence. We were created to have effective leadership on this earth. Notice that Adam and Eve were never commanded to dominate other people, but to dominate in life, through success, productivity, and influential leadership. I believe this explains the addiction many young people have to video games, because those games give them the thrill of winning; Yet, we were made to not just win a game, but to win in life.

This is what we were made for. The desire to be successful and influential is part of the Creator's original design – it's part of your DNA. It's not inherently evil, it's actually divine in origin. You were made for success and influence.

## 3. We are created to trust our Life Giver enough to obey Him.

When the Life Giver put the forbidden tree in the Garden of Eden, it was not to set them up for failure, but to put their trust to the test. Like any loving father, the Creator hoped His children would trust Him enough to take His words seriously. The tree was not a malicious mousetrap; it was a simple test of faith.

And the Lord God commanded the man, "You are free to eat from any

> tree in the garden; but you must not
> eat from the tree of the knowledge of
> good and evil, for when you eat of it
> you will surely die.
>
> — Genesis 2:16-17 NIV

Even today, the Creator wants us to trust Him enough to obey Him. To a certain degree, people are still searching for a God to believe in. Religion is a multi-trillion dollar business because people are longing for a deity to trust and follow. Why? It is our purpose to trust and love our Creator enough to obey Him; it is part of our original design.

## 4. We are created to enjoy empowering relationships.

The first human relationship Adam had was with his wife. Before Eve came into the picture, Adam slept next to a cat, talked to a dog, and rode on a horse. But then, the Creator brought a real, interpersonal relationship into Adam's life.

> The Lord God said, "It is not good
> for the man to be alone. I will make a
> helper suitable for him."
>
> — Genesis 2:18 NIV

God knew it was important for Adam to have a counterpart that he could share with. Adam was empowered in the vertical relationship he had with God, but the Creator knew that Adam also needed relationship with someone created like him. He was designed to be empowered through horizontal or interpersonal relationships as well.

Those who completely isolate themselves from others in order to have a deeper connection with the Creator are missing His intent. He designed us to enjoy empowering relationships. Eve was to make Adam a better man, and Adam was to make Eve a better woman. Relationships are for empowerment. Suppression, control, manipulation, betrayal, suspicion, hatred, bitterness, and heartbreak were never part of the Creator's design.

When a relationship functions according to the Creator's purposes, we read, "The man and his wife were both naked, and they felt no shame" (Genesis 2:25). This relationship had no pretense, deception, stress, or fear; they celebrated each other and how the Creator made them.

At our core, we all desire loving and empowering relationships because that's part of our original purpose. One of the harshest punishments rendered in the prison system is solitary confinement. It's so painful because it's so unnatural.

## 5. We are created for intimacy with our Life Giver.

Adam and Eve walked with the Creator. They went on special dates with Him. His presence was closer to them than the air they breathed. They knew His voice and had direct access to Him. In fact, Adam, Eve and the Creator were coworkers – partners!

> Now the Lord The Creator had formed out of the ground all the beasts of the field and all the birds of the air. He brought them to the man to see what he would name them; and whatever the man called each living creature, that was its name.
>
> — Genesis 2:19

There is still a worldwide desire to connect with the Creator! Although the German philosopher Friedrich Nietzsche declared, "God is dead. God remains dead. And we have killed him," the fact is that the Creator is *alive* in the hearts of people all over the world. People from every nation, tribe, and tongue are crying out for their Creator. They long to connect with the Life Giver because that was their original purpose.

## TRAGIC LOSS

Through humanity's rebellion against the Creator, humanity lost the unlimited potential of their general purpose! As a result, humanity as whole:

- Became sinners by nature and lost royal sonship.
- Became slaves to the devil, sickness, corruption, and misfortunes, instead of ruling in life.
- Became doubters who lost faith in the Creator and His commandments.
- Became distant from the Creator and dysfunctional in relationships.
- Became enemies of their Life Giver.

## THE MISSION OF JESUS CHRIST

But our story doesn't end here! Two-thousand years ago, a bold Rabbi would declare, "For the

Son of Man came to seek and to save the lost" (Luke 19:10). Some people think that Jesus came to start a new religion, but that's not true – Jesus Christ's mission was to restore us to our original purpose! He is the only One who can do it, because He is the *sinless* Son of God. Yet, even though He never sinned, He took on *our* guilt and brokenness and paid the price of death on the cross. He rose from the dead, and our purpose was restored to us.

Because Jesus completed His mission, our lost purpose has been redeemed and we can again walk in the original intent of our Creator! We can exchange our guilt and brokenness for His purity and wholeness. Though Jesus is so passionate to see you come into your original purpose, He will not force His way into your life. He will not restore your original purpose unless you want Him to. But when you say *yes* to Jesus Christ and receive Him as your Savior, then all that He came to redeem becomes redeemed in *your* life.

When you surrender your life to Jesus Christ there are some amazing benefits:

- You receive a new nature (2 Corinthians 5:17)!

- You now have the power to rule in life (Romans 5:17).

- You have the power of the Creator's Spirit living inside of you, which will empower you to trust in your Heavenly Father's love and keep the Creator's commandments (Romans 8:2).

- You have the power of the Creator's perfect love, which enables you to enjoy empowering relationships (Romans 5:5).

- Your access to the Life Giver has been restored; you're a partner with Him (2 Corinthians 5:18 & 1 Corinthians 3:9).

When you receive the gift of restored purpose from Jesus Christ, you no longer need to abuse your life by living contrary to your original design. Experience the saving power of Jesus! He wants to bring you into the true life you were created to live; this was His sole purpose for stepping into human history.

 **MEDITATION**

Are you living your general purpose?

# 13

# Your Unique WHY

As a magnificent piece of art reflects the glory of the artist, we become awestruck by the majesty of our Creator through the observation of creation (see Psalm 19:1-6 & Romans 1:20). From the intelligent single atom to the immeasurably vast galaxies, creation boldly declares the greatness of the Creator!

Because creation is a window through which you can see into the heart of the Life Giver, Jesus often used it to explain the Creator's intentions (see Matthew 6:26 -30).

God is so creative that you cannot find two people who are designed with identical fingerprints. Interestingly, even identical twins don't have the same fingerprints. Through the fingerprint, the Creator communicates the unique nature of each person's purpose. Somebody like you comes around once in eternity.

## No More Jealousy

Since no one shares the same exact purpose, jealousy is irrelevant. Jealousy is more than sinful; it's stupid. Jealousy doesn't come from an awareness of another's excellence and success; it comes from being ignorant of your own uniqueness and purpose.

Jealousy is as silly as an apple being envious of an orange, or an eagle being insecure because of a hummingbird, or a peacock competing with a parrot. Until we recognize that we have our own unique color, special flavor, one-of-a-kind build, and an irreplaceable contribution to make, jealousy will plague our lives and world.

Comparison can only lead to two destinations: jealousy and pride. When we get a true understanding of our unique purpose, the bridges to both destinations will be burned! If you are traveling upon those bridges, you will miss the Creator's destiny for you.

## RARITY + NEED = VALUE

An item's value is determined by its rarity and demand. For example, if the streets were paved in gold, gold would no longer be valuable. Or if gold smelled and looked like poop, no one would want it; gold would become irrelevant and without worth.

If pure drinking water was rare, it would be insanely expensive because of its relevance, for everyone needs drinking water. Aren't we grateful that it's not a rare commodity? But your purpose is a rare commodity.

Not only is your purpose one of a kind, but your purpose is also needed by an entire generation. You owe your generation the manifestation of your purpose. King David "served the purpose of God in his own generation..." (Acts 13:36). You have the same responsibility. This generation might not verbalize that they need you to fulfill your purpose, because they are not yet consciously aware of it, but they will become more and more aware as you shine forth your true self.

All of creation subconsciously demands that your purpose be fulfilled. This world really needs you! The Bible tells us, "For the creation waits with eager longing for the revealing of the sons of God" (Romans 8:19). Your purpose is absolutely rare and all of creation is crying out for you to fulfill it. You are a rare commodity in high demand – you are priceless!

Never question your value again.

 **MEDITATION**

Bask in the truth of your uniqueness and value.

# 14

# Useless Competition

Often, men do not compete with a woman in sports because they don't feel it is an even playing field. So we usually divide by gender in the arena of sports with men and women competing separately in the Olympics, golf, tennis, basketball, etc. But regardless of the gender, competition can get vicious!

Businessmen usually don't compete with pastors because their passion, vision, and goals are different. Most businessmen don't care about preparing and preaching the best sermons, but they often feel a spirit of competition toward other men who are in business – just like a pastor can fall into the temptation to compete with another minister.

An artist is probably not bothered by the success of a scientist because they are not in the same field. But artists can be aggravated by the success of fellow artists. I'm not saying those insecure feelings are right; I'm just staying that they happen. So, how do we put an end to them?

## Darwinism vs. Creationism

The Theory of Evolution teaches that everyone is a cosmic accident and without unique purpose. According to Charles Darwin, the "survival of the fittest" is an inevitable fact of life. This theory teaches that humans are not much different from animals (since they are our great ancestors), and therefore, like the animal kingdom, we ought to compete with each other to make it to *the top of the food chain* so we become the *oppressors* rather than *oppressed*!

According to evolution, life is one big competition where we attempt to out do everyone else and be the fittest that survives and thrives.

But the Creator's will was that we would *all* be successful in life (Genesis 2:16 & Romans 5:17)!

Evolution measures our success by how we do in comparison to others. But according to creationism, our success is measured by how we fulfill our divine purpose. Creationism says that life is not a competition; it's a conquest of your own destiny. If we all try to conquer the same hill, only a few can be on top and the rest will have to be below.

But the Creator has a unique mountain — or destiny — for each of us to climb. You have to reach the summit of your own mountain — your own purpose. Don't try to climb someone else's peak, and don't be jealous or threatened because somebody is getting close to the summit. Just as your purpose is peculiar to you, your passion, vision, and goals are exclusive to you. We can all be the king of the hill because the Creator has a hill just for you!

## YOUR OWN MOUNTAIN

Caleb asked his leader and comrade Joshua,

So now give me this hill country (mountain) of which the LORD spoke on that day, for you heard on that day how the Anakim were there, with great fortified cities. It may be that the LORD will be with me, and I shall drive them out just as the LORD said. Then Joshua blessed him, and he gave Hebron to Caleb the son of Jephunneh for an inheritance.

— Joshua 14:12-13 NIV

You have our own hill to conquer! I don't want your hill and you shouldn't want mine. Just like Caleb saw the mountain that the Creator purposed to give him, we need to see the mountain that the Creator has purposed for us.

- *What's your unique purpose?* What makes you different from others?

- *What's your unique vision?* What do you desperately want to see happen?

- *What are your unique goals? Specifically,* what do you want to accomplish while you are on this earth?

By answering these questions, you will get a good look at *your* designated mountain.

Only ignorant people compete. My climbing cannot negatively affect your climbing in any way. If your friend is reaching the summit of his mountain, it should only encourage you to keep climbing your mountain. Discouragement comes from comparison and competition, and it is a lie from the pit of hell.

I love to learn from those who have successfully climbed their mountains. Although their process and path will not be identical to mine, there are still principles from which I can glean. Don't point your rifle at the successful climbers; submit to their mentorship!

## Life is a Conquest, Not a Competition

If you see the conquest of your destiny as a corporate competition, you might be deceived into thinking that you are successful and have *made it* even though you are only one-tenth up your own mountain.

Instead of the spirit of competition, take on a spirit of conquest! When we compete and compare, it is a waste of precious energy. Paul, one of the history's most influential men, knew this very well. He wrote:

We do not dare to classify or compare ourselves with some who com-
mend themselves. When they measure themselves by themselves and
compare themselves with themselves,
they are not wise. We, however will
not boast beyond proper limits, but
will confine our boasting to the field
[or mountain] God has assigned to us.

> — 2 Corinthians 10:12-13 NIV
> (brackets added by author)

Some mountains may look similar, but none
are identical. Every destiny is as unique as the
snowflake. There are many who are called to
write, but no two written works will be the same.
A number of people are called to start churches
or outreaches, but no two should look the same.
Many are called to start businesses, but no two
businesses should be carbon copies of each other.

In a competition there is only one winner,
but in heaven, there are no gold, silver, and
bronze medals. Instead, you will be praised for
your faithfulness in taking your own mountain
(see Matthew 25:21-23). Therefore, are all win-
ners when we pursue our own purpose!

 **MEDITATION**

Take some time to throw off that spirit of competition and to identify and embrace your special mountain.

# 15

# All Champions

The Creator has a country, and it's called the Kingdom of God. When you've pledged your life to Christ, you become a resident of this great kingdom, and our culture is one of love, joy, and peace (see Romans 14:17). This is the country that needs to rule this world! The culture of the Creator's kingdom needs to uproot the culture of hate, greed, perversion, depression, and fear that is in our world.

## HOW DOES THAT HAPPEN?

As long as wicked people are sitting in places of influence, this world will suffer. In order to take these positions of power, we must do away with competition. We must realize that our countrymen are our comrades — our teammates — and we are all working together for the same goal: the advancement of the Creator's country. We must support and promote our fellow ambassadors (see 2 Corinthians 5:20).

> When the righteous thrive, the people rejoice; when the wicked rule, the people groan.
>
> — Proverbs 29:2 NIV

## HIDE, CRITICIZE, & MERCHANDISE?

As all the citizens of God's kingdom conquer their personal mountains of destiny and promote others to do the same, this world will be a better place. I've observed people intentionally try to keep others at the bottom of their hills. Because of their own insecurity, they try to keep other gifted people hidden. Instead of being excited as someone approaches the summit of their mountain — advancing the kingdom — they are threatened by the emerging leader.

When the citizens of the Creator's kingdom choose to live according to the inferior culture of this world, it has a devastating effect. When we are so threatened by the success of others, we keep others and ourselves small.

If every generation produces a leader of lesser quality, what will happen to our world in ten generations? But if we join with our countrymen and do whatever we can to help the next generation of leaders excel and thrive in their destiny, then in ten generations this world will become more heavenly.

It's sad when we choose to criticize our friend who is fulfilling their destiny and manifesting their potential. By the way, critics don't make history or leave a legacy; however, those they heavily criticize usually do. Which one do you want to be?

Have you been criticized? You're in good company. Have you been critical of others lately? You're in bad company. We gain nothing by having a critical spirit, but *everything* becomes possible when we help each other take our mountains.

This world will change for the better when all of God's people release their potential, manifest their purpose, and fulfill their destiny.

As creationists who believe in each person's purpose, we ought to endeavor to call out the hidden, dynamic leader in each person. We must be in the business of empowering leaders, not collecting followers.

Leaders who do not have passion to see the unique dreams and visions of those they lead come to fulfillment will just use people for their own purposes. This is selfish and shortsighted, because the Kingdom of God will only advance as every person fulfills their own God-given destiny.

 **MEDITATION**

Does your leadership reflect Darwinism or Creationism?

Do you rejoice over someone else's success? If not, why?

Is it your desire to raise up leaders and release them, or do you seek to increase the number of your followers?

Do you purposefully try to keep those around you suppressed, hidden, and less influential?

# 16

# Submission vs. Suppression

A two-headed monster is always ugly. A sports team, corporation, church, restaurant, etc, needs a responsible, wise leader who will cast vision and make final decisions. There must be some kind of leadership structure for an organization to run efficiently, and submitting to the appointed authorities requires humility and good character. While submission is beautiful, suppression is nasty.

If you lose your ability to dream big dreams, become conditioned to mediocrity, and start wasting your purpose in the name of submitting to your boss or church authority, you are robbing yourself of your own potential. Order in an organization is to maximize the potential of each person, not to prove Darwin's theory.

St. Paul explained that church leadership exists to help people find and fulfill their great purposes (see Ephesians 4:11-13). If your submission has led to suppression, something is wrong. Submission is designed to mature the greatness in you.

### HEALTHY SUBMISSION

The Creator's intent for submission is never to suppress; it's to maximize! The Bible teaches that wives are to *submit* to their husband's leadership, while husbands are to *love* their wives as Christ loves the church (see Ephesians 5:25).

What does Jesus' love for the church look like? While Jesus expects us to submit to Him, He is committed to seeing our full potential released! His leadership will not suppress you, but will cause you to soar to new heights! He loves you so much that He died to redeem your God-given destiny! A leader who is willing to give their life to see your potential maximized is a leader who is worthy of your submission.

## Wisdom for Servants

### 1. KEEP YOUR VISION

As you serve someone else, don't forfeit your own vision. When the nation of Israel demanded a king because they wanted to be like the other nations, the Creator knew it was not a good idea. He warned Israel that the king would take his subjects and make them slaves of his vision; everyone would become mere stepping-stones for his own personal ambitions. This was not the Creator's intent! He wanted each of them to learn and live their divine purpose. But the people of Israel insisted that they be given a king, and the Creator reluctantly gave them their request. Although a servant's heart is noble, we are to be kings in our purpose.

### 2. PROTECTION IS NOT SUPPRESSION

If your leader is not willing to give you everything you want right away, it does not mean that he is not interested in your potential; he might wisely be protecting you. Don't mistake protection for suppression. A two-year-old is not ready for a loaded pistol, no matter how badly he wants it. You may not be as mature as you think.

# Wisdom for Authority Figures

## 1. BE GENEROUS

Uncle Laban did not care about his nephew Jacob's purpose (see Genesis 29-31). Jacob was not just Laban's nephew; he was also his best employee. Unfortunately, Laban only cared about his own vision to grow his company and used his gifted nephew for his own benefit.

While serving under Laban's roof, Jacob felt used, unappreciated, unfulfilled, and restricted, but he continued to serve his uncle wholeheartedly. The Creator had to pull Jacob out of Laban's house, because no one can fulfill their purpose under Laban's style of leadership.

After Jacob left Laban, he flourished all the more – he fulfilled his destiny! If your leadership philosophy reflects Laban, don't be surprised if the Creator starts removing the best players on your team.

If you want to be a true leader, learn from Jesus, and be willing to do whatever you can to maximize each person under your care. May you have the wisdom and love to draw out the purpose and potential within each person.

> The purpose in a man's heart is like deep water, but a man of understanding will draw it out.
>
> — Proverbs 20:5

## 2. SUBMISSION IS GIVEN, NOT DEMANDED

If you have a heart to empower each person under your leadership, you will not have to demand submission. Don't demand that people submit to your leadership and serve your vision if you are not willing to give your life for their full potential to be released. This is no different than an abusive husband who demands his wife submit to him, or a disrespectful wife who demands love.

Don't demand people to do their part, especially if you aren't doing yours. Don't expect people to serve your vision if you aren't serving theirs. This generation will smell out your selfishness, and they will not run with you for long. Without their help, you will not be able to succeed in your vision.

## Corporate & Personal Purpose

I believe corporate destinies are realized as individual destinies are fulfilled and vise versa. Often, organizations and churches have not come into their destinies because they've not helped their members fulfill their personal destinies. If all the members of an organization are reaching the summit of their mountains, what would that do for the organization? It would thrive!

The flip side is also true; some people's dreams have not come to pass because they've not sown into the corporate vision of their organization or church. If you sow your purpose into your group and then the push your group's vision forward, then your purpose has moved forward! We need both personal and group vision; don't over-emphasize one at the neglect of the other.

 **MEDITATION**

Are you submitted to any leader or organization? Is this leader committed to maximizing your potential?

# 17

# The Manufacturer's Friend

I never took my Apple computer into the PC store to be fixed, and I did not try to find answers on Dell's website. If I have a problem with my Apple computer, I go to the manufacturer. If you are having a problem figuring out your purpose, go straight to the Manufacturer of your purpose.

Sony delivers their product to Radio Shack. Sony is the manufacturer, and Radio Shack is the retailer. Sony created the product and knows the product best, while Radio Shack's main role is to get the product out to the public.

The Creator is your manufacturer while your parents are your retailers. The Creator sent you to your parents so that they could clothe you, care for you, and present you to the world! But they did not manufacture your purpose! Therefore, the Scripture tells parents that "Children are a gift *of* the Lord" (Psalm 127:3).

Radio Shack does not write the manual for the Sony product because that is the manufacturer's job. The Creator, your Manufacturer, wrote a manual that is just about you:

> Your eyes saw my unformed substance; in your book were written, every one of them, the days that were formed for me, when as yet there was none of them.
> — Psalm 139:16 ESV

The Manufacturer knows your purpose and mode of operation perfectly! So if you aren't operating properly, don't look to your retailer or the other products that are shelved next to you; call out to your Manufacturer.

## THE WHY BEHIND THE WHAT

> He made known his ways to Moses,
> his acts to the people of Israel.
>
> — Psalm 103:7 NIV

The children of Israel knew *what* the Creator did, but because Moses had true *intimacy* with the Creator, he understood the *why* behind the *what*. Apart from intimacy with the Creator, you can only know *what* He made you, i.e. your height, ethnicity, skin color, personality, etc. But only through intimacy with the Creator can you fathom *why* He made you.

## HE WILL PULL OUT YOUR PURPOSE

In the Garden of Eden, the Creator brought animals to Adam so that he could name them. This speaks of partnership and teamwork, and it's what the Creator has always wanted. He didn't want Adam to fulfill his purpose apart from Him, but *with* Him. Adam and the Creator had so much fun as partners and friends.

Now the Lord God had formed out of the ground all the beasts of the field and all the birds of the air. He brought them to the man to see what he would name them; and whatever the man called each living creature, that was its name. So the man gave names to all the livestock, the birds of the air and all the beasts of the field.

— Genesis 2:19-20

When the Life Giver presented a nameless creature to Adam, Adam was presented with a problem to solve. As you grow in intimacy with your Creator, you will start noticing specific problems that are in the world; you will feel the very heartbeat of God and be moved with His compassion to bring a positive change.

Did you catch how amazing Adam's mind was? Adam not only named, but also *retained* the names of all the animals! For some, it is a challenge deciding where to go to eat. You probably can't even remember all the names of the people in your middle school.

Adam was operating on another level. The Creator asked Adam to name all the animals because He knew that Adam had the capability to do so, and Adam discovered something about himself when he met the challenge. The manufacturer knows the capabilities of His product.

When live in partnership with the Creator — in real intimacy with Him — He will pull out of you all the greatness that He put within you. He will pull out the magnificent purpose that He deposited within you! Those who are intimate with their Life Giver can't help but do exploits just like the One who made them (see Daniel 8:32)!

## LOVE PULLS ON PURPOSE

Remember, the Creator is love (see 1 John 4:16). So the Creator pulling out the potential and purpose within you is equivalent to His love pulling out the greatness in you! When you grow more and more intimate with Him, it will not be pride and selfish ambition that pulls out your great purpose and potential; it will be love and compassion! Books, songs, businesses, movements, teachings, millions of dollars, and so much more will be drawn out of you, because compassionate, divine love draws out your purpose!

When Jesus looked at all those who were suffering, He was moved with compassion and healed them all. The healing power within Him came out to heal the people Him – divine love pulled on His potential.

> And Jesus went throughout all the cities and villages, teaching in their synagogues and proclaiming the gospel of the kingdom and healing every disease and every affliction. When he saw the crowds, he had compassion for them, because they were harassed and helpless, like sheep without a shepherd.
>
> —Matthew 9:35-36

 **MEDITATION**

What will you miss out on if you do not have intimacy with your Creator? How are you pursuing that close relationship with Him?

# 18

# **Pinpoint Your Purpose**

The following three questions can provide helpful clues to pinpoint your purpose.

## **1. When do you feel most alive?**

Fish are energized as they swim. Birds thrive as they fly. What makes you come alive? Jesus told His disciples, "My food is to do the will of

Him who sent me and accomplish His work" (John 4:34). As Jesus Christ fulfilled His pre-ordained purpose, He was divinely energized. You will find energy you never thought you had when you find your purpose.

Recently, I taught at my church for about seven hours a weekend. People asked me if I was wearing myself out. Physically it was tiring, but out of all the jobs I've done at church (which is everything except women's ministry), nothing gave me more energy and satisfaction than teaching truth. Why? Purpose.

When you connect with your purpose — even if you are only serving a few people — you will enjoy what you do. I'm not saying that there won't be a desire to expand the boundaries of your influence but even if there aren't thousands of people flocking around your purpose, you will still enjoy it. And as you enjoy yourself, more people are drawn to your purpose.

## 2. What is your gravitational pull?

Here's an interesting question: Can people who have not yet been born-again and received the Creator's Spirit still find their purpose? The answer is yes. They can gravitate toward their purpose. Moses gravitated toward his purpose as a deliverer before he knew the Creator. Paul gravitated toward his purpose as a gatherer and teacher before he was born-again. Peter was inclined toward leadership and public speaking before he received the Creator's Spirit.

If you are born-again and Spirit-filled, what did you gravitate to before your new birth and infilling?

If you are not yet born-again and Spirit-filled, what have you found yourself being pulled toward?

Even when I was a lost, rebellious teenager who was disconnected from the Creator, I've always had an inclination to listen to people's problems and look for practical solutions. I'd be on the phone for hours, counseling my friends and trying to get to the root of their problems. Many years later, I'm still trying to get to the root of problems. In fact, this book was born out of a burning desire to sever the root of jealousy, competition, boredom, laziness, and the unfulfilled life.

Those who receive the saving work of Jesus Christ, and consequently become born-again and then Spirit-filled, will come to a greater awareness of their purpose because they become more sensitive to their spirit. Our purpose is embedded in our spirit. Our spirits are in a dead state before our rebirth (see Ephesians 2:1), but when we are energized with the Creator's very Spirit, we receive a clearer understanding of our purpose and a greater boldness to pursue it (see John 14:26 & Acts 1:8).

## DIVINE SIGNALS

Whether spiritually dead or alive, every human is given a conscience from their Creator that can pick up some divine signals (see Romans 1:21 & 2:4-5), so everyone can potentially pick up clues about their purpose.

It's important to know that just as our conscience can be seared through continual abuse, our sensitivity to purpose can also be seared through abuse. Your conscience is abused when you continually violate it, and your purpose radar is abused when you embrace a poor self-image, selfishness, and drunkenness.

If you keep saying to yourself, "I can't ever do anything right!" You are abusing your purpose radar, and your ability to receive a divine vision for your life can be short-circuited.

If you continue to thing about yourself and focus on how to please your selfish desires, your purpose-radar is being abused, and you can grow deaf to the voice of your purpose.

If you are always intoxicated on entertainment, jumping from one party to another, addicted to drunkenness, you are abusing your purpose radar, and you will drift farther and farther from your divine destiny.

## SATAN'S MISSION

Satan doesn't want anyone to fulfill their purpose, so he works extra hard to keep people from finding it. Satan wants to crush everyone's purpose radar so they will stay lost. But more than anything, Satan works to keep people away from Jesus Christ. He does not want you to be born again or experience the infilling of the Creator's all-wise Spirit.

Satan is your enemy and he is very afraid that you will find your purpose. He is on a three-fold mission to kill, steal, and destroy (see John 10:10), but your God-given purpose has a three-fold plan to impart life, share goodness, and bring restoration to your generation!

## 3. What Moves You?

One of the most prolific preachers of all-time, Charles Spurgeon, once said, "A winner of souls must first be a weeper over souls." Before we can be effective in our destiny, we need to weep over the very thing we are purposed to fight. Your tears are trails to your purpose. What brings tears to your eyes?

What have you found yourself fighting against? Food fights against hunger. Water fights against thirst. Books fight against ignorance. Phones fight against disconnectedness. Vitamins fight against deficiencies. Your purpose will also fight against something. What is the problem that your purpose is designed to demolish?

Like other teachers, I can't stand ignorance. The Scripture that reads, "My people are destroyed for lack of knowledge..." (Hosea 4:6) causes my heart rip apart. I have an unquenchable anger toward ignorance. Thus, I've invested my own finances to create teaching materials, and I teach the Scriptures with all my heart. My holy anger compels me to fulfill my holy purpose.

Every world-changer knows anger, and Jesus Christ was no exception. It is important to note that Jesus never physically hurt anyone, but He clearly expressed His holy anger. Those who know the Creator will know holy anger, and it will lead you to your holy purpose. One primary purpose of Jesus was to restore the Creator's honor, which is why He drove out the money-changers in the temple and turned over the tables; they were dishonoring the Creator's house.

> In the temple he found those who were selling oxen and sheep and pigeons, and the money-changers sitting there. And making a whip of cords, he drove them all out of the temple, with the sheep and oxen. And he poured out the coins of the money-changers and overturned their tables. And he told those who sold the pigeons, "Take these things away; do not make my Father's house a house of trade."
>
> — John 2:15-17

 **MEDITATION**

According to what makes you weep and what makes you angry, describe your purpose.

# 19

# What About My Job?

Many people work jobs in which they find very little fulfillment. That's why so many live for the weekends. I hear "Thank God it's Friday!" much more often than, "Thank God it's Monday!" The more you realize your purpose, the more difficult it can be to work a job that is seemingly unrelated.

How can you go from just working a job to living by purpose? Maybe you are extremely frustrated because you are possessed by your divine purpose, but because the need to make ends meet, you don't have the time, energy, or opportunities to fully pursue your destiny, as you desire.

If you can relate to this inner tension, the Creator has five wisdom keys that will encourage you and help you make a glorious transition from working a job to living your purpose.

## KEY 1

### Catch the Creator's heart over a specific issue.

Nehemiah received news that the city of Jerusalem was struggling and despondent. This report of a devastated Jerusalem pierced Nehemiah's heart, causing him to weep over the city he loved. We read his emotional response over Jerusalem's shame:

> When I heard these things, I sat down and wept. For some days I mourned and fasted and prayed before the God of heaven.
>
> — Nehemiah 1:4

What is the issue in our world that unlocks your fountain of tears? What makes you so sick to your stomach that you lose your appetite? What do you find yourself passionately praying about? These questions can lead you to your purpose. Nehemiah did not just weep and pray over the problems, he did something about it. Your tears and prayers mark the beginning, not the end.

## KEY 2

### Don't prematurely quit your job.

His heart was boiling with passion and he was consumed with purpose, but Nehemiah continued to do excellent work at his job in the king's court though it was unfulfilling. Being wise, Nehemiah didn't ditch his job prematurely. He patiently waited until the Creator opened the door for him to pursue his purpose.

Just because you've found your purpose doesn't mean you should automatically quit your job! Continue to work there until your Creator specifically commands you to leave your job or opens another door for you to walk through. Meanwhile, work your job with a spirit of excellence. Nehemiah even did his best to hide his heartache over Jerusalem, because he didn't want his burden to take away from the quality of his work. That's a fine employee. The Bible teaches that God promotes faithful workers, not lazy bums. When God sees it's time for you to be further released into your purpose, He is smart enough to make it happen for you.

For a season, the Creator may leave you in a job that is not directly associated with our purpose. Trust Him, and remember that He wants you to walk and be successful in your purpose even more than you do!

The Creator often uses the job to further clarify His vision in you and build your character so you will be equipped for your purpose, instead of butchering it. Additionally, He is also waiting for you to develop a spirit of excellence so you won't be a flaky worker when you are released into your purpose. Develop the spirit of excellence now, so it will be second nature as you walk in purpose.

## KEY 3

### Articulate your passion and purpose.

One day, the king confronted Nehemiah about the sorrow in his heart that he was trying to conceal.

> And the king said to me, "Why is your face sad, seeing you are not sick? This is nothing but sadness of the heart." Then I was very much afraid.
>
> — Nehemiah 2:2

Losing his job and not having any income frightened Nehemiah, and it still scares people of purpose today. Yet, God made it all work out. Nehemiah was able to make a living and still pursue his purpose! You can believe that God will do the same for you!

When the King asked Nehemiah what was on his heart, Nehemiah had a clear answer to give him:

> I said to the king, "Let the king live forever! Why should not my face be sad, when the city, the place of my fathers' graves, lies in ruins, and its gates have been destroyed by fire?"
>
> — Nehemiah 2:3 ESV

You, too, must be able to articulate your purpose and holy anger; the Creator's vision for your life must be crystallized in you. Sometimes God will wait until His passion and plans are more matured in you before He will release you into your purpose.

## Key 4

## Receive Divinely Inspired Goals.

> Then the king said to me, "What are you requesting?" Then I prayed to the God of heaven.
>
> — Nehemiah 2:4 ESV

If Nehemiah had answered the King's question with, "I don't know," he would have been unable to fulfill His purpose. Instead, he first prayed to the Creator and *then* answered the King saying:

> If it pleases the king, and if your servant has found favor in your sight, that you send me to Judah, to the city of my fathers' graves, that I may rebuild it.
>
> — Nehemiah 2:5 ESV

Nehemiah was able to share his burden and *also* a plan. After you've identified your purpose, then you need to establish prayerful goals. Your holy anger has revealed to you *what* you want to change, but *how* are you going to do it? It's important to have practical goals – a game plan.

Don't be that person who always has an opinion and some great vision, but you never have a plan; you just have a nebulous idea of what you want to happen. Create a proposal that explains how you are going to see this vision become a reality. If you don't have a strategy, it is very unlikely that your purpose and passion will effect any change.

Through prayer, Nehemiah received a divine game plan that he was able to share with the King. As we prayerfully seek God, He will deposit inspired goals into your spirit. The psalmist wrote, "Delight yourself in the LORD, and he will give you the desires of your heart" (Psalm 37:4 ESV). Plans and goals should not take the place of prayer; they must be born out of that place of intimacy.

Set prayerful goals related to your purpose. Receive divinely inspired goals for the next month, the next six months, the next year, the next two years, and the next five years. Those who have a plan and goals will always accomplish a whole lot more than someone without them.

## KEY 5

### Expect supernatural favor.

> And the king granted me what I asked, for the good hand of my God was upon me.
>
> — Nehemiah 2:8

The next thing you know, Nehemiah was on the next available trip to Jerusalem with all his needs taken care of. The Creator will move on the hearts of people to support your vision and open doors for you. The king gave him such favor because the hand of the Creator was upon Nehemiah. When the divine hand of blessing is upon you, nothing can stop you from fulfilling your purpose! Your divine purpose is born of the Creator, blessed by the Creator, and backed by the Creator.

Have you caught the Creator's vision for your life? Is His compassion your fuel? Are His plans your roadmap? Then expect unexplainable fa-vor to mark your life! When you are fully pregnant with your purpose, the Creator will move upon the hearts of influential and powerful people to help you manifest your great destiny. I'm a living witness that these five keys will unlock your purpose.

If you have a love for the Creator, then He will work all things together for your good. Experiences at your previous jobs will not go to waste. St. Paul wrote, "And we know that for those who love God all things work together for good, for those who are called according to his purpose" (Romans 8:28).

Keep loving God and He will take the good, bad, and ugly from your past and use it all for re-demptive purposes. The Creator has called you for a great purpose, and He will work things out for you – just keep loving Him and cultivating that personal relationship with Him.

 **MEDITATION**

Write down some of your God-inspired plans and goals, which will help fulfill your purpose.

121

# 20

# Believe in Your Purpose

If you don't believe in your purpose, neither will others. If you see yourself as having nothing to offer, others will view you the same way. Moses sent twelve spies to scope out the land, which the Creator promised to give them. Ten spies came back intimidated by the giants who occupied the land. Scripture records their negative report to Moses:

> And there we saw the Nephilim (the sons of Anak, who come from the Nephilim), and we seemed to ourselves like grasshoppers, and so we seemed to them.
>
> — Numbers 13:33

## How Do You See Yourself?

In this passage of Scripture, we see that how you view yourself is often how others will perceive you. Many people go through rejection after rejection because they see themselves as a reject. Your inner world will create your outer world. What you believe will be made real in your life; you attract what you carry. If you carry the confidence that you are a powerful person of purpose, you will eventually attract such treatment.

Jesus Christ knew *who* He was; He saw Himself as a man of purpose, and soon others began to catch on. If you carry around a loser identity, you will be treated like a loser and attract those who live low lives. But if you see yourself as an honorable person, you will attract honor and honorable people.

I've been blessed to have world-class leaders pour into me and support me as they recognized my potential. But I made it easy for them to recognize my potential, because I recognized it first!

If I kept denying my potential, I'd be a waste of time for others to pour into. My negativity would have punctured holes in my cup, causing whatever others poured in, to just leak out – I would have been a poor investment.

If Jesus did not believe in His own purpose, His disciples would not have believed either. But Jesus was willing to die for His purpose, and His disciples followed suite.

Just as Jesus had a strong team that helped Him fulfill His purpose, I'm convinced that the Creator will connect us with people who will sow into our destiny. People will sow their time, money, prayers, etc. into your purpose once they see that you are passionate and walking in it.

The Creator only sent Adam a helper (Eve) after he had received his purpose and started working it. The Creator will send the right people to help you fulfill your purpose after you believe in your purpose and start working it.

## WRITE & PREACH YOUR PURPOSE

If you go to the bank for a business loan but have no clear vision for your business, then why should they approve the loan? Why should people sow into your vision, if you don't have a clear picture of what that is? You need to "Write the vision; make it plain on tablets, so he may run who reads it" ( Habakkuk 2:2). Writing your vision will help clarify your goals inside of you, so you can clearly communicate them to others.

Jesus Christ was not ashamed of preaching His purpose. He boldly declared why He had come to earth and what He was all about. Others began to believe what He believed about Himself. We, too, need to preach our purpose. What is preaching? It's a declaration what you believe. It's not a suggestion, a proposal of possibilities, or a roundtable of opinions; it's the bold proclamation of what you believe is fact! When you boldly proclaim what you believe about your purpose, others will begin to believe what you believe.

Yes, some might label you as arrogant and others might laugh at you, but you will also attract the right people who will support your purpose and partner with you to see your vision become reality.

 **MEDITATION**

In only one or two sentences, write a concise purpose statement. Then, using only two paragraphs, write a personal vision statement, which you can declare to others.

# 21

# **Confidence From Faith**

Watch out for this thought: "I can't be very confident because I have not accomplished anything yet." The Scriptures admonishes us to walk by faith and not by sight (see 2 Corinthians 5:7). You might not see the full manifestation of your purpose yet, but you are still to walk around believing that you are significant.

Jesus taught that if you want to manifest what you desire, you have to believe that it is already a done deal.

> What things soever ye desire, when ye pray, believe that ye receive them, and ye shall have them.
>
> — Mark 11:24 KJV

You have to believe in your destiny as if it's already accomplished.

## WHAT ABOUT PRIDE?

There is nothing wrong with thinking highly of yourself. The Bible warns, "I say to everyone among you not to think of himself *more* highly than he ought to think, but to think with sober judgment" (Romans 12:3 ESV).

When people think of themselves *more* highly than they ought to, they begin to treat people poorly, and that is unacceptable. There is nothing wrong with believing you are significant, as long as you don't ever believe that others are less significant. If think your purpose and gifts are *more* important than someone else's, you've crossed the line, and you are thinking of yourself *more* highly than you ought. But there is nothing wrong with seeing yourself as the Creator sees you – that's seeing yourself with sober judgment.

You can be confident in your own purpose, destiny, and calling because it's God's grace that has given them to you. But once you think that your mountain is more significant than somebody else's, you've entered into sheer arrogance. A humble man sees everyone's mountain as significant.

> If anyone thinks he is something when he is nothing, he deceives himself. Each one should test his own actions. Then he can take pride in himself, without comparing himself to somebody else, for each one should carry his own load [climb his own mountain].
>
> — Galatians 6:3-5
> (brackets are author's)

Be confident, not arrogant!

## OVERCOME INSECURITIES

John the Baptist fulfilled his purpose and stepped into his destiny as he baptized Jesus, even though he didn't think he was qualified. John didn't think he was worthy but, because Jesus told him that he must baptize the Messiah, he stepped out and did it. Humility says, *"Jesus, Your view of me is greater than my view of myself. Therefore, I'll do what you call me to do, despite my feelings of unworthiness."*

Jesus' understanding about our purpose and destiny is much weightier than our opinions. His high calling for you is greater than your low opinion of yourself! Therefore, don't let your insecurities kill your purpose – let your purpose kill your insecurities!

 **MEDITATION**

What is the difference between confidence and arrogance? In which do you walk?

# 22

# Fans, Foes, & Field

When you become a firm believer in your purpose, you will see three groups of people: your fans, your foes, and your field.

There was a reason why everyone was drawn to a young Hebrew man named Joseph —he was a man who saw himself in light of the Creator's purposes; he carried a dream from the Creator. As you see yourself as a person of purpose, you will attract fans and foes. Your fans will celebrate your purpose, and your foes will seek to destroy it. In the process, you will also locate your field: those the Creator has called you to serve. Let's talk about each one.

## YOUR FANS

Your fans are those who endeavor to promote you. When Joseph served in the prison, the jail warden became a big fan and promoted him to manage the prison. Pharaoh became a fan too and promoted Joseph to be his second-in-command. Fans do not compete with you – they celebrate you. They see the gold in you. Thank God for fans!

Don't you want to be a fan that celebrates a person's purpose instead of criticizing them? Don't fortify a person's weaknesses – pull out their treasures. Be a fan.

Joseph's fan base started very tiny and remained small for a long time. But then, almost overnight, his fan base grew to millions. Here we are thousands of years later, and I'm also a fan of Joseph. Don't be discouraged if your fan base is small right now; just keep living out your purpose. Treasure the few fans you do have, and that number can explode overnight as you just stay on track.

## YOUR FOES

Personal purpose has a unique way of instilling value and confidence within a person. However, a person who is possessed by purpose often bothers insecure people. They will write you off as arrogant and ambitious, as Joseph's brothers did to him, and they might try to discourage you, giving you all the reasons you are "unqualified." Remember, even Jesus' own siblings and hometown of Nazareth did not celebrate His God-given purpose. They mocked, belittled, and laughed at Him. But just as Jesus was committed to His purpose, you must be as well!

Since Joseph was his father's favorite, he became the least popular among his brothers. Your foes are those who are jealous of you because they are competing with you. Joseph stood for integrity, and his brothers were disgusted by his high standards. Your foes are disgusted by your strengths instead of appreciative of them.

Joseph's brothers wanted to kill him but, instead, sold him off to be a slave in Egypt. Your foes want to kill your dreams and potential and see you live a low-life. They won't promote you, but they will criticize and try to hide you.

Your foes are the people who want to control you. Potiphar's wife had the "hots" for Joseph, and she flattered him with her sexual advances. While she gave the impression that she was really into him, she was really just into herself. Her agenda was to use Joseph for her own satisfaction.

There are selfish people out there who will act like they are your fans, but they just want to use you for their own benefit. They don't really care about *you*, only what you can do for them. They are foes in fan's clothing.

When Joseph refused to sin with Potiphar's wife, she turned on him, falsely accused him of rape, and sent him to jail. There are people who will only appreciate you if you let them control your life. They want to squeeze you into their selfish mold and will throw you to the dogs if you don't obey them. They might act like your friends, but they aren't – they are your foes.

People are designed to grow into their divine purpose, not be squeezed into the mold of another person's expectations. There are controlling, manipulative people out there, so you must be committed to your personal purpose; you don't want to become the play-dough of controlling people instead of the masterpiece of the Creator!

Although your purpose will attract foes, don't be afraid of them. In Joseph's case, the Creator caused the horrible treatment from his brothers and Potiphar's wife to work together for Joseph's good. Just love God and don't fear your foes, because the Creator promises to work it all for your good and His purpose (see Romans 8:28).

If Joseph wasn't sold into Egypt as a slave, he couldn't have fulfilled his destiny. If Potiphar and his wife didn't send him to jail, he wouldn't have become Pharaoh's right-hand man and fulfilled his grand purposes. If you stay true to your God-given purpose, the attacks of your haters will backfire!

The schemes of Jesus' haters backfired too, and it led to the payment of our sins, His glorious resurrection, and, now, He has more followers than ever!

## Your Field

Your field is the group of people that your purpose needs to serve. Let's call it your mission field. Some people get so bitter and hurt by their foes that they refuse to keep serving their field. Joseph didn't fall into that trap, and even though he had reason to be bitter and selfish, he continued to serve all the people who came into the prison.

One day, he met the Pharaoh's ex-baker and ex-butler who had just been fired. He served them by asking about their problems and even accurately interpreting their dreams for them. Joseph prophesied that the ex-butler would be restored to office, and then he asked him for a favor, "Only remember me, when it is well with you, and please do me the kindness to mention me to Pharaoh, and so get me out of this house" (Genesis 40:14).

Instead of returning the favor right away, the butler actually forgot about Joseph. Serve your field, but don't live for their appreciation, because there will be times when your field will just take you for granted! There will be times that it feels like your time is wasted by serving them, but keep serving your field!

I believe that God tests us during the silent years – when the field fails to appreciate you. God wants to know if you will still love the people and be faithful to your purpose. So don't blame your field for taking you for granted or forgetting about you, just keep loving and serving them.

After two silent years, the butler finally remembered Joseph and connected him with Pharaoh, who desperately needed a dream interpreted. In prison, Joseph interpreted dreams as a volunteer, but now Joseph was interpreting a dream because his gift was in highest demand. There might not be an immediate demand on your gift, but keep volunteering to serve your field. A tipping point is coming!

As Joseph interpreted Pharaoh's dream (faithful in his purpose), he stepped into his destiny. Like Joseph, your field can take a quantum leap from two people to millions if you stay faithful to serve your field.

If you want to reach your destiny, be thankful for your fans, don't fear or become bitter toward your foes, and keep serving your field.

 **MEDITATION**

Currently, who are your biggest fans and foes, and what is the field that God has called you serve?

# 23

# Develop & Protect
# Your Purpose

When the Creator placed Adam in the Garden of Eden, He made Adam responsible to *develop and protect* the land and animals. The Creator didn't have Adam share the garden with ten thousand other people. It was Adam's domain and Adam's responsibility. Your purpose is your domain and your responsibility.

## DEVELOP YOUR PURPOSE

Eden literally means *delight*. You will find much delight in developing your purpose! How do you cultivate or beautify the domain of your purpose? One of the primary ways is to perfect your gifts; your gifts cannot be separated from your purpose. The development of your gifts becomes equivalent to the development of your purpose. Those who neglect their gifts are practicing bad stewardship of their purpose.

King Solomon wrote, "A man's gift makes room for him and brings him before the great" (Proverbs 18:16 ESV). Nothing will spread the scope of your influence like the development of your gifts. It is not your charm or academic credentials that will impact those of prominence; it will be through the perfecting of your God-given gift.

Solomon also wrote, "Whoever works his land will have plenty of bread, but he who follows worthless pursuits lacks sense" (Proverbs 12:11). To live a prosperous life, you must develop what you have been given: your domain and gifts. Those who waste time on developing things unrelated to their purpose are wasting their own potential!

I know individuals who are broke because they keep pursuing paths in which they are not gifted. If they would just work what they have been given, they would thrive. The Creator has given each of us the power to make wealth, and that is by giving us relevant gifts. Develop *your* Eden, not somebody else's garden! Your success in life depends upon your alignment to your purpose.

When I first discovered that the Creator had purpose for me to be a preacher and teacher, I started preaching to the birds and teaching the trees. This might sound silly, but I had to start somewhere. I would preach with tears in my eyes, and would feel the power of the Creator surge through my body; sometimes I could hardly stand. I'm sure that I had heaven's attention as they looked down and saw a young teen possessed with purpose. Before I was publishing books, I wrote over three hundred meaty blog entries. I was developing my Eden.

## PROTECT YOUR PURPOSE

Now, it's not just *developing* our Eden, but also *protecting* our Eden. Satan is afraid of your purpose, because when the Creator's children

— who reflect His nature — begin working their purpose and spreading their influence, Satan's strongholds will be overthrown by the culture of heaven. Satan will do anything to discourage and distract you from your purpose. He will try to deceive you into thinking you don't have a destiny. He will try to convince you that you are unimportant or unqualified to pursue greatness! He will get you distracted with worthless pursuits.

Therefore, all the more, you need to protect your destiny and stay resilient in your God-given purpose. Every person who has lived out their God-given purpose, had to withstand the ambush of doubts, pull through the storms of discouragement, and had to stay focused in the midst of the fog of distractions.

There will be times when the only two beings that believe in your purpose are you and the Creator. There might times when nobody will be there to encourage you and you are going to have to encourage yourself in the presence of the Creator. When people turned their backs on King David, there was no one to encourage him except his Creator. This was enough for David because he saw himself and his Creator as the majority!

And David was greatly distressed, for the people spoke of stoning him, because all the people were bitter in soul, each for his sons and daughters. But David strengthened himself in the LORD his God.

— 1 Samuel 30:6

 **MEDITATION**

What are you presently doing to develop your gifts?

# 24

# Serve Your Gift

As soon as you discover your gifts, begin to use them so they become strong. Your gift is like a muscle; it develops with use. Your gifts are weapons of purpose. Master these weapons by practicing them – as you master your gifts, you will master your purpose. Find an organization or a church where you can serve in your gifts; volunteer to serve others in an area that exercises your gift, and then watch it flourish!

True servanthood is not only washing the dishes or vacuuming the church floors; it's serving your gift to your generation. Jesus of Nazareth was the model servant, and He did more than wash feet. Jesus served the world by sharing His gifts and fulfilling His potential! Washing dishes, vacuuming, and volunteering to be an usher has its place and is virtuous, but don't forget to serve your generation by serving your gift and living your purpose!

You rob yourself and others when you allow insecurity and fear to stop you from sharing your gifts with others. Your gift will not grow if you never go beyond your comfort zone. Get over your fears; serve someone with your gifts, and as you do, you will serve your way into greatness. Jesus said, "Whoever would be great among you must be your servant" (Matthew 20:26 ESV).

## WHAT POURS OUT OF YOU?

Let's take a look at a fascinating story in the Old Testament:

> Now the wife of one of the sons of the prophets cried to Elisha, "Your servant my husband is dead, and you know that your servant feared the LORD, but the creditor has come to

take my two children to be his slaves." And Elisha said to her, "What shall I do for you? Tell me; what have you in the house?" And she said, "Your servant has nothing in the house except a jar of oil." Then he said, "Go outside, borrow vessels from all your neighbors, empty vessels and not too few. Then go in and shut the door behind yourself and your sons and pour into all these vessels. And when one is full, set it aside." So she went from him and shut the door behind herself and her sons. And as she poured they brought the vessels to her. When the vessels were full, she said to her son, "Bring me another vessel." And he said to her, "There is not another." Then the oil stopped flowing. She came and told the man of God, and he said, "Go, sell the oil and pay your debts, and you and your sons can live on the rest."

— 2 Kings 4:1- 7 NIV

This woman was in crisis. She was about to lose all that was dear to her, and she didn't know what to do. The creditors are a picture of the devil and his demons, who are in the business of stealing from the Creator's precious people (see John 10:10). She was overcome with feelings of powerlessness and that's when the prophet Elisha asked her a simple question that would solve her dilemma – "What have you in the house?"

She replied, "Your servant has nothing in the house..." Now, if that was all she said, the creditors would have robbed her and she would have died a miserable woman. But, she added, "...except a jar of oil." Elisha recognized that that oil was the solution! That oil represents the gift that the Creator has put inside of you.

This woman was able to go from powerless to powerful by recognizing what was in her house. The ability to live a powerful and influential life is already within you. But if you say that the Creator placed nothing of value inside of you – you are not gifted – then Satan will steal from you!

He will attempt to kill your legacy. He will take away your children – those you should have mentored. No one enthusiastically submits to the mentorship of someone who is broke, depressed, and powerless. Recognize that there is a gift inside of you. When you identify that gift and serve it to others, you will see divine power flow out of you! You have something to pour out.

## WHOM DO YOU POUR INTO?

The widow became a very wealthy woman after she recognized her gift and stepped out to pour her gift into empty vessels. Those empty vessels represent the bankrupt hearts and real needs of our world. When we compassionately meet the needs of broken people, the Creator puts His *super* to your *natural*, and what will flow from your life will be nothing short of *supernatural*.

When the Creator's compassion is in our hearts, His power is demonstrated through our lives. Apply this right away, and you will be shocked out of depression! Stop wallowing in self-pity and complaining that your life has no significance or future – go find people to pour your gift into!

Don't isolate yourself; you have too much to offer. King Solomon wrote, "Whoever isolates himself seeks his own desire" (Proverbs 18:1 ESV). There are too many needs to meet, problems to solve, and people to love for us to hide in our shell.

World-renown motivational speaker and government consultant, Dr. Myles Munroe has written over sixty books. When I asked him how he was such a prolific writer in the midst of running five businesses, leading the largest church in his country, and speaking all over the globe, he responded that it was a combination of two things: gift and love. The gift was *from* the Creator, but the love was *for* the people. The gift was always within him and could not grow dormant, because compassion for people pulled on the gift and unleashed a life-giving river!

After breaking out of poverty and into prosperity, the widow was able to mother her sons, which represent those you mentor. As you recognize your gift and pour it into others with a servant's heart, you will become that mentor you were destined to be, and you will find much fulfillment as you empower others to go even further than you!

 **MEDITATION**

Whom do you pour into? Which of their needs are you meeting?

# 25

# Help Others into Purpose

Do not be deceived: God is not mocked, for whatever one sows, that will he also reap.

— Galatians 6:7

It was the Creator Himself, who instituted the principle of sowing and reaping. If we assume that what we harvest will be different from what we plant, we mock God.

If we think we can intentionally restrict the potential of others and yet somehow fulfill our own potential, we are mocking the Creator. The Scriptures warn:

> Whoever digs a pit will fall into it, and a stone will come back on him who starts it rolling.
>
> — Proverbs 26:27 ESV

This proverb warns us against trying to limit or harm another person's potential. If you put someone in the pit of discouragement or try to roll a stone that crushes someone's hope, you will end up the biggest loser.

Jesus gave a stern caution that "Whoever says to his brother, 'You good-for-nothing,' shall be guilty before the supreme court" (Matthew 5:22 NAS). He never wants us to kill the potential of another by causing them to believe they are worthless. Everyone is valuable.

Jesus harshly rebuked the Pharisees for being white-washed tombs full of dead men's bones (see Matthew 23:27). The Pharisees used religion to kill the potential of their followers. They didn't impart life and energy to the purpose of others, but only death to their divine dreams. The Pharisees condemned instead of encouraged and suppressed rather than empowered.

Choose to be the person who empowers others. Cheerfully give what you can to further someone else's purpose. If that's the kind of heart that you have, the Creator promises to supply ample grace for you to fulfill your own destiny.

> Each one must give as he has decided in his heart, not reluctantly or under compulsion, for God loves a cheerful giver. And God is able to make all grace abound to you, so that having all sufficiency in all things at all times, you may abound in every good work.
>
> — 2 Corinthians 9:7-8

It's understood that you can't help everyone, but you *can* help someone. Ask the Creator to show you whose purpose you need to support, and how you can best help.

## CHANGE THE CULTURE

If your organization, church, or family is full of competition, jealousy, and lack of encouragement, it has become a graveyard for potential. Do whatever you can to turn the culture of your group into one that empowers, encourages, and elevates! It can start with you. Make your organization the maternity ward for divine dreams! Be the culture changer. Be the revolutionary. Sow your time, encouragement, prayers, love, and even finances into seeing purpose realized in those of your group.

Never blame others for not sowing into your vision; focus on your own sowing. Bitter criticism does not create a positive culture of empowerment and success – it fortifies disempowerment and failure. Correct a problem by responding with the opposite spirit. If the people around you are not encouraging, don't just complain, be the most encouraging one in the bunch!

If you've been faithful to serve and sow into another man or woman's vision, when you are fully impregnated with your vision from the Creator, you can expect many people to come alongside to help you. But if you've been a selfish lone ranger, don't be surprised if the only one working to see your vision fulfilled is you. That's a lonely road.

 **MEDITATION**

Whose purpose are you assisting? Have you sown your money, time, and encouragement into their purpose?

# 26

# Run
# with Divine Ideas

Every great invention started with an idea. Running with an idea can make or break your life – it depends on its source. If you act on an idea from the devil, you can end up in prison or worse. The travesty of events in New York City on September 11, 2001, started with one demonic idea. But, imagine what can happen if you will run with a divine idea?

## UNLEASH THE HIDDEN POWER

There are ideas that flow out of your spirit and pop into your mind. These thoughts flow from your purpose, which is embedded in your spirit. Only when you act upon your idea can you release its potential!

A young teenager heard an ugly giant named Goliath taunt the armies of Israel, and a divine idea sprung to his mind, "I think I can kill this giant for the glory of God!" If David had not acted upon this thought, he would have wasted the potential within that divine idea. You know the story, he acted upon the thought and fulfilled destiny by killing Goliath.

## SEIZE THE MOMENT

As Peter saw his rabbi walking toward him on the water, the divine idea popped into his head that he, too, could walk on water. He quickly asked Jesus to bid him come. Jesus gave the OK, and Peter made history as he walked on water.

Now, if Peter had waited a month before he decided to jump on that idea, it would have been too late. He seized his divine moment so it became a defining moment in history!

On the day of Pentecost, another divine thought crossed Peter's mind, "I should get up and preach to this huge crowd about Jesus Christ and explain this outpouring and manifestation of the Creator's Spirit." This thought was born out of Peter's purpose, and as he seized the moment, three thousand souls were born-again. He did not let fear of failure or fear of man abort his divine thought. That's a lesson for all of us.

There are times when the Creator specifically breathes on an idea and that's exactly when you need to jump on it. Miracles happen when you seize those divine ideas. Just like how an angel stirred the waters of Bethesda once a year and the first person who seized the opportunity was healed (see John 5:1-5), I believe that when God stirs an idea in your heart, that would be the opportune time to plunge into it.

Have you ever heard the phrase, "You missed the opportunity of a lifetime!" Sadly, it happens far too often. The prophet Elisha told the King of Israel to strike the ground with his arrows, and when the king only struck the ground three times, Elisha was irate! He yelled at the king saying:

You should have struck five or six times; then you would have struck down Syria until you had made an end of it, but now you will strike down Syria only three times.

— 2 Kings 13:19 ESV

Elisha was angry because the king failed to take full advantage of the divine moment. During this interaction between the prophet and the king, there was a divine window of opportunity that needed to be seized. If the king had only discerned the moment of opportunity and passionately seized it, he would have experienced much greater success.

Bringing this story down to our world, I believe that the prophet Elisha is a picture of God's Spirit, and the king portrays you – you are purposed to reign in this life (see Romans 5:17). The Spirit of the Creator will give you divine ideas, but you need to passionately run with them, instead of just passively flirting with them. This will determine how much you accomplish with your life.

As a writer, there are certain messages that begin to stir in me and that is when I need to capture them, just like you would capture a memorable moment with your camera. I had divine enablement to write on certain topics during certain times. I seized those ideas as they seized me.

Presently, I'm fired up about the topic of personal purpose. This book you are reading started as a divine idea. The thought of having a concise book about personal purpose, which would set people free boredom, insignificance, depression, jealousy, competition, and ineffective leadership, began to excite me! The Spirit stirred the waters of my heart so I captured the idea and enthusiastically ran with it.

The fact that you're finishing this book is proof that there is potential in those simple ideas that flow out of the personal purpose in your spirit. There can be millions of dollars, deliverances, healings, miracles, and salvations behind one God-inspired idea. But you must start somewhere and do something to unleash the potential of that idea!

King Solomon penned, "In all labor there is profit, but mere talk always leads only to poverty" (Proverbs 14:23 NASB). Starting *somewhere* is the step that most unfulfilled underachievers never get to. Don't let your divine ideas die incarcerated in the prison of your fears, doubts, and laziness. Run with them.

 **MEDITATION**

What divine ideas are stirring inside of you? How will you seize your moment?

# 27

# **Bounce Back From Failure**

Have you ever blown it so badly that you thought you were now disqualified from reaching your destiny? Have you made such horrible mistakes that you felt like God had abandoned you? Some feel that they are damaged goods because of the wrong decisions that they have made, and they have given up on their divine dreams and visions. They no longer feel worthy to pursue their purpose. Discouragement, condemnation, and shame have paralyzed them.

There is a time and place to call people to a life of integrity, but there is also a time and place to encourage people who have failed. This is the time and this chapter is the place.

I remember watching one of the "Rocky" films and Rocky's opponent hit him so hard that he hit the floor. Blood was flowing from his mouth and his eyes looked like plums. It didn't seem like he would be able pull himself up from the canvas, but then he heard the voice of his trainer, yelling at him to get up! At that moment, he did not need an hour lecture on how to dodge punches; he needed some encouragement! He needed to know that the fight was not yet over! Rocky was strengthened in his heart, the energy flowed to his body, and he miraculously won the bout.

This last chapter is not an hour lecture, but a heartfelt cry to those who have fallen and think they can't get up – it's not over! Get up, for you can still win!

## PETER HITS ROCK BOTTOM

Jesus' lead disciple Peter knew what it was like to fall hard. He denied Jesus not once, not twice, but thrice. You may have been able to shake off your guilt when you messed up the first time, but perhaps this time it is difficult to forgive yourself because you've repeated the same foolish decisions again and again. That was Peter's predicament – he had walked with Jesus for three years and knew better than to deny Him publicly. After Peter realized what he had done, he wept bitterly.

Jesus prophesied greatness over Peter, and Peter had big dreams that had blossomed in his heart since following Jesus. Yet, after betraying his Rabbi publicly, he gave up on his dreams of being a great spiritual leader and went back to fishing.

One day, while he was fishing, Peter saw a man on the shore, and as soon as he realized that it was the resurrected Jesus, he put on his robes, jumped into the water, and began to swim to Jesus (see John 21:7)! I have two questions: why would you wear garments before taking a swim? And, wasn't he ashamed to face Jesus?

## Robes of Righteousness

I don't have a logical reason why Peter dressed to swim, but I do have a spiritual one. There is a profound message in Peter putting on his robe to pursue Jesus. The Scripture reads:

> I will greatly rejoice in the Lord; my soul shall exult in my God, for he has clothed me with the garments of salvation; he has covered me with robes of righteousness.
>
> — Isaiah 61:10

Peter putting on his garments is a picture of what we need to do when we have failed. Put on the robe of righteousness that Jesus purchased for you on the cross. In other words, recognize that Jesus died on the cross for your sins in order that you might be made "the righteousness of God in Christ" (2 Corinthians 5:21).

This robe of righteousness is not a license to sin, but a license to bounce back from failure. Receiving this robe will take away your shame, and instead of running from Jesus, you will swim toward Him! When you understand that you have righteousness, which is not earned, but a gift that Jesus purchased for you on the cross, it will cause passion for Jesus to grow inside of you! You will swim as fast as you can to Jesus and grow in your relationship with Him. He will restore your sense of purpose and re-commission you into your destiny.

## PASSION, NOT CONDEMNATION

During the interaction between Peter and Jesus, Jesus did not hammer Peter with accusations. He didn't put Peter on the spot and ask, "Why did you betray Me... after all I've done for you?" Instead, Jesus asked Peter a simple question, "Simon, son of John, do you love me more than these?" Jesus repeated this strategic question three times.

Do you see the motivation of Jesus' heart? Instead of dumping the weight of condemnation on Peter's shoulders, Jesus stirred Peter's love for Him! Shame will keep you down, but love will cause you to bounce back! When you fail, it is not Jesus' desire that you hate yourself; He wants you to love Him more! Jesus imparts passion, not condemnation.

Thanks to Jesus, Peter went on to fulfill his destiny and live his divine purposes. His legacy lives on today.

### JUDAS' FATE

Like Peter, Judas also made a serious mistake and sold out his Rabbi for thirty pieces of silver. After Judas realized what he had done, he wept bitterly as Peter had, but then he went on to make an opposite choice: he hung himself on a tree.

After you make your mistakes, you can be like Peter and put on the robe of righteousness and pursue Jesus with all your heart, allowing Him to rekindle your love for Him. Or you can follow the course of Judas – you can wallow in condemnation and shame, and choose to hang your potential, destiny, dreams, visions, goals, and purpose!

Maybe you are at this very fork in the road. I plead with you; follow in the way of Peter! Your life is not over yet! Get up! You can still win!

As a kid, I remember riding my roller blades down a fast hill. I kept looking at a car that was parked on the curb and saying to myself, "Whatever you do, don't hit that car!" After rehearsing that statement in my head about three times, Bam! I hit the car.

Our focus becomes our destiny. While Peter was led to focus on the mercy of the Lord, Judas fixated upon his own depravity.

## DAVID'S TRIP UP

King David lusted after Bathsheba, the attractive wife of Uriah who was one of David's most respected and loyal soldiers. He didn't control himself and ended up committing adultery with her. She got pregnant, and to cover up the adultery, David resorted to killing off faithful Uriah. David broke half of the Ten Commandments: he coveted, he committed adultery, he lied to cover it up, he stole somebody's wife, and he murdered! That's bad.

King Saul, David's predecessor, didn't finish his homework and only partially obeyed God's orders. God fired Saul! God restored David! Does this make any sense? Most religious people would have fired David and kept Saul, right? Yet God's ways are above our ways, for God always looks at the heart.

Saul's life tragically ended in wasted potential, while David goes down in history as a man who fulfilled his divine purpose (see Acts 13:36)! Why? Saul and David both messed up badly, but while Saul's heart was set on building a name for himself, David's desire was to know God's heart (see Acts 13:22). Even when Saul blew it, he just wanted his reputation back, but David wanted his relationship with God back.

Although David had to suffer some consequences for his actions, God still kept all the promises that He made to David, and David left a legacy. As long as you have a heart for God, God can work with you.

So you made some mistakes, do you want to end up like Saul or David? It all depends on the quality of your heart. Do you have a heart for God or not? Peter sinned against Jesus, but did not lose his heart for Jesus. Judas sinned against Jesus and forfeited his heart for Jesus. David sinned against God, but didn't give up on his love for God, while Saul sinned and no longer cared about his relationship with God.

When David was confronted about his sin, the prophet Nathan told him that although he would suffer the effects of sin, his sins were already pardoned. If you have a real love for God, that heart will lead you to real repentance, which brings real forgiveness. What's more important than the failures of your yesterday is your heart for God today.

## LOVE WILL SAVE YOUR LIFE

Ten seconds are left on the clock of the basketball game. Your team is down by one, and you're given the opportunity to make the last shot. The clock is ticking... and with four seconds left, you fire... and miss. At the sheer frustration of your miss, you end up pounding on the floor, and the other team gets the rebound – the game is over. That was Judas' story.

However, let's say you missed the shot but hope filled your heart so you went for the rebound, put back the shot, and your team won the game! That was Peter's story. If you have a heart for God and don't allow condemnation to kill your hope, the ball will bounce your way, and you will be in position for the rebound and the put-back.

God's heart is always to restore us, not condemn us. He knows that condemnation only makes your heart grow cold and calloused. Reject the road of condemnation! Walk the road of renewed passion, and love for your Life Giver. Allow His grace and mercy to clothe you, and pursue Him wholeheartedly again! Choose love. For when you choose love, you will walk in true repentance, which leads to true forgiveness, and aligns you for true restoration. Peter's love for Jesus enabled him to bounce back from his failures. David's love for God led him to restoration.

Only when you love God, can God work all things together for your good.

> And we know that for those who love
> God all things work together for good,
> for those who are called according to
> his purpose.
>
> — Romans 8:28

God couldn't work things out for Judas or Saul because they didn't have love. Yet, if you have a real love for God, He can even use your failures to fuel your passion and compassion. He can turn your mistakes into ministry, and He will enable you to fulfill your destiny! No matter how badly others hurt you or you hurt yourself, don't ever lose love, for love is the key to unlock your purpose. Don't lose the key.

You may have lost a battle, but never lose your love. Love beckons you to bounce back from any and every kind of failure. Love gives you the will to live your *why*. Love resources your reason and preserves your purpose. Love is the greatest commandment from the Creator and thus, the greatest sin is to lose a heart of love. God's love *for* you is the greatest hope for your purpose; God's love *in* you is the greatest hope for your destiny, and God's love *through* you is the greatest hope for humanity.

 **MEDITATION**

Will you follow in the way of Peter and David, or Judas and Saul? Be honest with yourself; do you still have a heart for God?

# ABOUT THE AUTHOR

**DANIEL H. PARK** has been teaching since he was fifteen years old. Ministering in many churches, conferences, youth events, and revival meetings in the U.S. and abroad, Daniel teaches with insight, clarity, creativity, and compassion, delivering life-changing understanding and timely prophetic messages. He ministers with sensitivity to the spontaneous flow of the Spirit, and many have been equipped, healed, delivered, and have experienced the undeniable presence of God through his ministry.

Daniel has authored several books, which are being used as curriculum by youth, college, and young adult ministries, as well as adult small groups.

Daniel and his wife Meg both serve as Junior Trustees (18-35) for Dr. Myles Munroe's International Third World Leaders Association.

For more information, visit:
**www.danielhpark.com**

Or contact Daniel at:
**pastordhp@gmail.com**